From the Handler's Post

Competitive Strategies and Training Tips for Sheepdog Trialing

Vergil Holland

OUTRUN PRESS

FROM THE HANDLER'S POST. Copyright © 2015 by Annemarie Holland. All rights reserved. Printed in the United States of America. No part of this book may be used or reproduced in any manner whatsoever without written permission except in the case of brief quotations embodied in critical articles and reviews. For information address Outrun Press, 1764 Millstone River Road, Hillsborough, NJ 08844.

Cover photo by Carol Clawson.

ISBN-13: 978-0-9965996-0-3
ISBN-10: 0-9965996-0-6

Library of Congress Control Number: 2015946699

Contents

Introduction (by Susan Carvalho)	i
1. The Philosophy of Stockdog Competition	1
2. The System of Classes in Stockdog Competition	7
3. The Outrun	25
4. The Lift	47
5. The Fetch	59
6. The Turn at the Post	97
7. The Drive	109
8. The Pen	125
9. The Shed	145
10. The International Shed	173

Introduction

by Susan Carvalho

It is a great challenge to reduce to words all of the intangibles that go into sheepdog training and trialing. On the one hand, as any of us knows if we have had more than one dog, every dog is an individual. What works swimmingly for one dog might do harm to another, and unless you want to go through a lot of dogs trying to replicate the one that you trained well, you have to adapt to this amazing array of difference. On the other hand, there is also that tricky thing called "feel." So much about dog training has to do with sensing the level of the dog's frustration, the sheep's tolerance, and the balance between new learning and reinforcement.

It is a rare person who can master these challenges, to train dog after dog to the highest level and to nurture and maximize all the talent that a young dog promises. It is even rarer to be able to transmit that knowledge—again, to an array of handlers from seasoned trialers to novices with their pet dogs, and everyone in between.

Vergil Holland was that kind of teacher. Like so many new handlers, I showed up with my pet border collie Kelsie on a leash, and my jaw dropped when I saw what he could do with his dogs. I thought, "We will certainly never be able to do that!" But in his trademark way that all who knew and loved him recall, Vergil broke it down into parts, talked about taking baby steps and "not putting your dog into college before she was done with kindergarten," taught us to watch our sheep and how to listen to a dog, and celebrated with us when we won that first Novice ribbon as if it were the Finals. He was as proud of his students as he was of his own wins, and that is because of how he valued the role of teacher and mentor.

Hundreds of students have attended his clinics, taken lessons, sat under the tent and heard him comment on a run, and gained tremendous insights as a result—insights about that dog, dogs in general, training, and communication. But while only a few handlers have the gifts to become effective trainers, even fewer can find a way to corral that knowledge into written form.

Donald McCaig, in *Eminent Dogs, Dangerous Men*, captured this difficulty when he wrote that "communion and communication intertwine at

♠ FROM THE HANDLER'S POST ♠

their roots." As a handler who knows my limitations, I was often frustrated when our lessons would move into that realm of talent and feel; I wanted rules and formulas that I could study, master, and execute. Border collie training sure doesn't offer that! Sometimes you need to lean in, step back, modulate your voice, make a hundred tiny adjustments that help your dog. How can that be communicated at all, let alone in writing? Again, Donald McCaig in *Eminent Dogs:* "You cannot train a sheepdog if you have too great faith in words."

And while Vergil was in many ways a master of language, the written word was not his thing. He didn't have the time to read a lot, and seldom wrote more than what fit on a notepad. But he loved a good book on tape—especially on a roadtrip!—and had that keen intelligence that meant that, if he heard a word once, he owned it. So as a teacher, he often paused to find exactly the right word that would convey a complex thought or an intangible meaning. This richness of expression—appreciated all the more now that he is gone—is what made him able to be not just a trainer, and not just a teacher, but someone whose wisdom could be conveyed in texts: first in his training manuals, then in the long-selling book *Herding Dogs: Progressive Training*, and in the many articles he published in the *Working Border Collie Magazine*.

♠ VERGIL HOLLAND ♠

I met Vergil in 1993, when he moved to Versailles, Kentucky. Early in our friendship, I began to work with him on finishing the book manuscript and on the WBC articles. It was a match of complementary skills—in gratitude for the work on the book, Vergil gave me my first talented border collie, Laurie.

Even before the book came out, Vergil was already thinking about the next one: a handbook for trialers that we called *From the Handler's Post: Tips, Tricks, and Training Tools for Winning Stockdog Trials*. From the beginning, Vergil's focus was clear: handlers needed a deep toolbox of strategies developed through their training programs, and then they needed to know which ones to draw on at particular crisis points on the trial field. We started a WBC series called "My run fell apart when . . ." because, as he often said, "the run didn't have to fall apart then—if the handler had known what to do, and if the dog had the right foundational training program."

I never knew how handy my medical-transcriptionist training would be for this work we would do together! We met periodically, with the cassette player between us. Sometimes we would sketch a rough outline of topics together, or he would bring one in hand; at other times, I would start asking a series of questions to start him talking. What I remember most is the

♠ FROM THE HANDLER'S POST ♠

faraway look he would get when trying to capture those intangibles: his way of finding the right words was to put himself back out on the training field or the trial field, and feel his way through the dilemma. Then he drew on his rich vocabulary in that way that he often did during a lesson or clinic, looking for exactly the right words to convey to others something that was so innate to him.

My transcription process wasn't literal—because of the wandering nature of our taped conversations, I generally rearranged the pieces, sometimes connected sentences or wrote transitions that, hopefully, contributed to the readability. Then he would review, edit, catch where I might have misconstrued his meaning, or fill in something that didn't come across as clearly as he would like. *The Working Border Collie* format was ideal for us to color in that outline that was supposed to become *From the Handler's Post.*

Life got in the way, as it often does, and we didn't complete the book. I am so grateful to Outrun Press for gathering these items and producing the book, even though he would have loved to have the chance to finish it and to enjoy it. Now that he's gone, too soon, when I re-read these articles I wish they had been pure transcription, so that that voice coming through would be more truly his. Even better, I wish we had these lessons in a series of videos, to watch him get that faraway look and reach for just the right word to communicate something so intricate and inexplicable.

Vergil left a lot of himself behind, in his friends and all those he mentored. Some of it is here, in these pieces that convey his overall philosophy that successful trialing is the product of a careful and balanced foundation of training. He would be proud to know that his list of successful students continues to grow.

1

The Philosophy of Stockdog Competition

As a trainer, I see a lot of people come through my gate for the first time. Some are trained competitors with trained dogs; some are trained handlers with new dogs; some are untrained handlers with trained dogs; and many have no training either on themselves or on their dogs. Over the years, watching this diverse group sort itself into hobbyists, short-term fans of the sport, or real "trial addicts," I have had the opportunity to discuss and think about what it is that hooks us, that makes us travel all those miles, start over again with all those dogs, and keep striving for that next high placing or, in rare instances, that next win.

Most people do not get into this sport with the idea that they want to compete. In fact, most are not even sure that they want to train their dogs. I would say that the most typical beginner scenario is that a person walks in with a black-and-white dog that he or she does not know what to do with, that might want to do something with sheep. Often this dog is a high-energy, frustrated, ill-behaved dog, because the owner did not know quite what he was getting into when he decided to get "one of those smart dogs."

In rare cases, this novice dog takes right to the idea of working sheep; the owner's eyes open wide as the dog's instinct rises to the surface, and within days or weeks the dog is transformed from pet to partner. In these situations, the owner happens to have hit the jackpot. More often, however, the dog is half-hearted when he starts out, but it's the owner who gets hooked. This owner will spend weeks, even months, coaxing the instinct to the surface, trying to get her dog to do what she sees those distant cousins doing. Generally, the dog slowly progresses, but rather quickly the owner starts thinking about and looking for that second dog, one that is bought with more of an eye toward proven working bloodlines, toward a promising future in stockdog training and, perhaps, toward trial competition.

Of course, stockdog trialing used to be dominated by stockmen. Those who used their dogs on a daily basis fell naturally into competition, to finding out who had the best dogs and to

♠ FROM THE HANDLER'S POST ♠

breeding and training ever better dogs. But as traditional farming styles have diminished and four-wheelers have taken over the pastures, and as the popularity of the border collie breed has grown, those who used to be called "hobbyists" or "amateurs" have increasingly become the mainstay of the sport. Part of what addicts us to trialing is the fact that a dedicated hobbyist with a good dog can, eventually, compete with the "masters," the stockmen and full-time farmers. Trialing has become less a test of endurance and more a test of precision, of training and teamwork, such that handlers with other primary occupations but who really put energy into practicing, training on different fields, trialing in as many different situations as possible, and learning from the professionals, can present a real competitive threat even to the top handlers. Anyone can win, on a given day, with the right training foundation, the right dog, and the right set of sheep. Of course, mileage and experience give a tremendous advantage to those who dedicate a large portion of their lives to the sport, but due to the interaction of so many intricacies and variables, newer handlers can compete quite well in many situations against the professionals. This is part of the reason that so many people who might start out only dipping a toe into this pool end up diving right in and not coming up for air!

♠ Vergil Holland ♠

As we have said, many are drawn to the sport not because of their love of stock or of competition, but because they are fans of the border collie. They have learned to appreciate either the intellect or the athletic ability of the border collie, perhaps through obedience, flyball, or agility training. But working stock establishes a different kind of relationship with the breed. While some border collie-oriented competitions probe the depths of the border collie's athletic ability, they do not fully engage the thinking processes of the dog. Agility and flyball involve a tremendous degree of precision and timing, but training happens in a matter of months. Herding involves a more technical kind of teamwork, which takes years to maximize, and which teaches the handlers to understand, in a profound way, the thinking processes of the dogs.

Of course there is a flip side to these rewards. In stockdog training, progress is measured in inches rather than yards. Trialing also constantly presents different kinds of challenges—different breeds of sheep, new terrains—that continue to test and stretch the ability of the dog-handler team. There are many people who don't really want a thinking dog, who would rather have a set of rules and written guidelines, so that in each new city and each new situation they know more or less what

♠ FROM THE HANDLER'S POST ♠

is coming and how to prepare for it. The very scope of trial competition, its infinite variations, frustrates some beginning handlers, and they drift back toward other types of canine training or sport. This level of challenge keeps stockdog trialing from growing more quickly than it does, but it is also this level of challenge that makes the sport so very appealing to those who do stay with it.

Finally, I think what surprises those who enter this sport and what keeps them drawn to it is how deep the minds of these dogs go. In other types of canine training, the dog's mind is asked to go only so far; no more is required than drive, desire, talent, and habit. In comparison with stockdog trialing, only a small percentage of the dog's intellectual depth is plumbed. But the farther we go into stockdog training, the more we realize that we have not yet fully understood the dog's potential to respond, to react, and to partner with us. Even after almost thirty years in this sport, I continue to be surprised and amazed at the potential that different dogs show, and the challenge of finding the training approach that might best maximize that potential. There is always room to teach more to your dog, and to learn more from your dog. You never reach the final goal.

For this reason, stockdog training involves developing a much closer relationship with your dog than the one you might create through other kinds of training or competition. It changes your way of looking at your dog, but it also seems to change people in a much more profound way. It changes how we look at farming, and how we look at stock. And eventually, as we get more involved in this kind of work, it can change the way we look at people and at life. It teaches us that everything can't be cut-and-dried; it helps us understand how to work with many individual minds, individual wills, individual instincts, of which you need to be the interpreter and the coordinator. That level of challenge and excitement gets extremely addictive.

2

The System of Classes in Stockdog Competition

The Novice Class in Stockdog Trials

In border collie trials, the Novice-Novice class exists so that people who have not been trialing or handling dogs for very long can get started in competition. When I began competing with border collies, everyone started in the Open class. There were many problems with that system: it was intimidating, it was expensive, it was time-consuming for the people hosting the trial, and most of the time, the dog was in over its head—not to mention the handler. Novice handlers felt very insignificant, to the point that many people who worked with border collies never started in competition at all. For these reasons, I think it is extremely helpful that the class system developed, with beginning and intermediate levels of competition alongside the Open class.

It is important for both the dog and the handler that certain goals are met before the two of you enter your first competition, even at the Novice-Novice level. I have hosted and judged many trials, and I am always surprised that, with all the avenues of information available to beginning handlers, they do not really know what to expect and how to prepare for their first competitions. Since I too have been in "Novice shoes," I know how important it is that this first time on the trial field be a good experience for both dog and handler. For that reason, I would like to outline a few recommendations about what you should know, and what your dog should be able to do, before that first time on the trial field.

When I am judging, or talking to Novice people, I often find that they have no idea what the rules of competition are. Part of the reason for this is that the USBCHA intentionally is not rule-bound, especially at the lower levels; it leaves the specific design and running of the trials up to the local organizers. I very much support this stance. However, there are certain general guidelines that are in effect at all trials, guidelines that have to do with how the outrun is

♠ FROM THE HANDLER'S POST ♠

done; at what point(s) the handler may leave the post without being disqualified; what the handler can or cannot do at the pen, and what comprise the basic elements of the course. If possible, the ideal way to learn these rules is at a judging clinic. It is a widespread misconception that judging clinics are aimed toward handlers who are in training to become judges; however, this is not the case. Judging clinics are intended to teach handlers how points are deducted on the trial field: for example, this type of error generally costs two points, or that mistake may cost up to five points. These seminars are very useful not only for instructing yourself about the basic rules of a trial, but also for helping you to think about strategies, about which mistakes are more costly than others. In my opinion, there are far too few judging clinics offered in this country, and the ones that do exist are poorly attended.

 The ideal Novice course gives the dog and handler enough time to gain control of the situation, to settle down and to show what they know. Novice handlers may travel a substantial distance to a trial; they pay a sizeable entry fee, and they deserve the time to do more than a gather and a pen. Shorter Novice courses do not always ensure that the best dog wins; rather, the best-penning dog generally wins. For these reasons, I advocate that Novice courses always include at least a wear, during which the handler can work his dog up close and regain more control before the pen. I have strong objections to trials that shorten the Novice course in order to save time; it is important for us as "professionals" and Open handlers to realize that these Novice handlers are the future, and they deserve the same competitive consideration as we expect for ourselves.

Since there are very few rules determining who may run in which class, handlers need to make their own decisions about the level at which to run their dogs. Handlers who are new to trialing should not let their egos get ahead of their dogs and should not move up too quickly. Most clubs and associations will allow you to drop down a class if you buy a dog that is running above your experience level. This is a necessary step in your own training process, and you should avail yourself of it, for as long as you need to do so. By the same token, when you know that your dog has advanced and you are a more seasoned trialer, you must exhibit some "trial etiquette" and move up to where you belong.

No matter where they start, Novice handlers make a huge mistake when they head into their first trial with the intention to win. We all enjoy competition, and we all want to see our dogs perform at their best, especially in public. But

♠ FROM THE HANDLER'S POST ♠

Novice handlers, in their first trials, should have only one thing on their minds: to keep things under control, so that the experience is a good building-block in their dog's training. There is plenty of time for competition later on. At this stage, you need to go to the post with a very real plan for what might go wrong and how you will handle it. You need to anticipate problems; to be ready to leave the post if you need to whether or not this means disqualification; to be ready to help your dog out of a troublesome or out-of-control situation. You need also to realize that your dog probably will not perform at the level he has shown at home. On a new field, the pressures are different, the sheep are new to the dog, and the atmosphere of tension can really affect the way your dog works. This means that he will probably run a little bit faster, push a little bit harder, listen to you a little bit less. And if you are not prepared for that situation, your young dog will quickly become "ring wise," to use an equestrian term. The dog will realize that he can get away with things on the trial field that he cannot get away with at home. You need to be prepared to prevent this realization on the part of your dog. Of course, you are not at the trial to "train" your dog; training is to be done at home. Nevertheless, you should do your best not to permit anything that will allow bad habits to develop in your working dog at this level—even if this means sacrificing the competition aspect of the trial. Help your dog find the sheep if necessary; keep your dog from circling the sheep at the top; and keep the sheep from splitting apart during the fetch.

There are certain basic skills which you should teach your dog before the first trial. One important maneuver to practice is gathering sheep that are held by another person and dog. I have spoken to innumerable handlers who do not practice this before their first trial, and they do not even realize how confusing this situation is to the young dog. This should very definitely be practiced at home, at very close distances at first, so that the dog is not caught off-guard or does not lock onto the spotter when he rounds the top of the outrun and finds a person and dog there.

Another talent that you should help your dog to develop is running on a different field. If a big trial is your dog's first working experience off his own training field, your run quite likely will be disastrous. The dog needs to be taught to read the field, to read new pressures, and to use the skills you have so carefully taught him. Ideally, your training program will involve travelling to different sites or different flocks of sheep. If it does not, it is my strong recommendation that you take the time to compete in

♠ FROM THE HANDLER'S POST ♠

regional "fun day" competitions before your first "real trial." At fun days, you are often allowed more liberties than at a trial with time constraints and other pressures. Often you may leave the post to help your dog; you can walk part of the way to the sheep before sending your dog; the judge may give more helpful hints than he would at a trial; the other handlers may be more congenial and relaxed; and in general, both you and your dog will leave feeling satisfied and confident.

Other preliminary skills include the following. At a minimum, your dog should be able to do a 100-yard outrun and fetch, in a controlled manner and under command, in either direction. You should be able to stop him at the top of the outrun, so that you can collect your thoughts and he can collect his. You should be able to flank your dog during the fetch to some degree, even if he will not be pulled all the way around the sheep; otherwise you are in real danger of losing the sheep at a trial. Once the sheep are brought to you, the dog must also understand how to bring the sheep *around* you, because you will need to wear the sheep either to a set of panels or directly to the pen. Flank commands and keeping his distance from the sheep are fundamental to this skill. Finally, you and the dog should have practiced some work at the pen, at least enough so that the dog understands the objective.

If you feel that you need your dog on a leash on your way from the gate to the post, then you probably do not have the necessary control on your dog to make for a successful trialing experience. In my opinion, new handlers should use this as a guideline or yardstick on their training. If your dog tries to leave your side, or cannot be called off the sheep, more homework probably needs to be done before you begin competition. If you need a leash on your dog as you go to the gate, then you should do so, particularly with nervous or high-strung dogs; otherwise, the amount of control that it takes to keep them with you can put them in the wrong frame of mind once you do get on the field. Once you are through the gate, you should be able to walk anywhere and know that the dog will not leave your side. If you do not have control at a distance of three feet, you will not have control when the dog is 100 yards away working sheep.

Off the training field, there are other preparatory measures that can make your first trial an encouraging and fun experience. Just as you should attend some trials as a spectator so that you can get accustomed to the atmosphere, your dog needs to feel comfortable in crowds and in public areas, where people might be

♠ FROM THE HANDLER'S POST ♠

shouting and other dogs are walking around everywhere. He needs to be used to travelling, to being tied to a vehicle or trailer or crated for extended periods of time, to behaving himself and not getting uptight in unfamiliar situations.

Another point I would stress to beginning handlers is the importance of the handlers' meeting which takes place immediately before the start of the class. These generally informal meetings are not only the judge's opportunity to state his expectations, but also the handler's opportunity to ask questions. You should not be afraid to ask *everything* that is on your mind. You should find out what the judge's policy is if you need to leave the post. You should ask how stringent you need to be about the turn around the post. If you have questions about scoring or about the course, this is the time to ask. This may feel like an intimidating situation, but as a judge I can assure you that the meeting exists to allow you this opportunity, and that you have the right to understand the fundamental rules of competition before you get to the post.

The Intermediate Levels of Stockdog Trials

By the time you are ready to compete at the Pro-Novice level, your dog should be on whistle commands at least to some degree. At many trials, the distances on the course will necessitate that you at least be able to stop your dog and to call him off with a whistle command. You and your dog should also be quite proficient at driving the sheep, in whatever pattern may be decided for that particular trial.

Discussion of the "typical" Pro-Novice course brings up a point that I consider to be of fundamental importance in the system of classes. Trials which only offer the three-tier class system encompass a huge variety of dogs and handlers in the Pro-Novice group. Some dogs, and/or their handlers, might have just recently moved up from the Novice class and they are not ready for a long drive involving three legs and extended distances. As a stepping stone, the ideal course for these handlers is a drive through one panel, with perhaps a short crossdrive through a second set of panels. Other handlers may be almost ready to move into Open-class competition. For these reasons, I am a strong advocate of the intermediate class currently called Ranch or Open Ranch.

In fact, I have a hard time understanding why opposition to the widespread adoption of this class of competition still exists, when there are so many good arguments in support of it. Primarily, I feel that most dogs, and relatively novice handlers, are not ready for Open-level

♠ FROM THE HANDLER'S POST ♠

competition simply because they have mastered the Pro-Novice course. Open classes involve two elements that require a huge leap from the Pro-Novice level: one is the level of competition, and the other is the number of potential variables in the course and sheep. In terms of competition, we need to consider the technical skill level required and the expense associated with running competitively in today's Open classes. An advantage of this is an increase in the size of the purse. However, this often happens at the expense of the newer handlers, who may compete for many for months or even years before reaching a skill level to win prize money. A system like this does not encourage handlers to stay in active competition.

Course variables also contribute to the enormous gap between Pro-Novice and Open classes. The variety in Open class courses is challenging and enjoyable for handlers who are prepared for it, and who have trained their dogs in such a way that they are not in over their heads. An Open class may involve an outrun of up to 600 yards; it may involve a split as well as a shed; it may include a Maltese cross or other challenging obstacles; and it can involve working very difficult sheep. It takes several years for a handler to develop the kind of versatility and technical ability necessary to be competitive at this level, yet I would not recommend that a handler and dog remain at the Pro-Novice level for such an extended period of time.

Of additional consideration is that many new handlers get a dog trained to the upper-Pro-Novice level, and then start a second dog. If these handlers have moved up to the Open class too quickly, they cannot start these second dogs in Novice competition which, as relatively new handlers, they may still need to do. A handler competing at the Open Ranch/Ranch level is still able to start a second dog in Novice.

These are the primary reasons that a transitional class between these two levels has become a necessity. The only argument that I hear against including this "Open Ranch" course is from some older handlers, who say that they started right in Open competition without undue hardship, and therefore new handlers should go through the same initiation process. For that matter, I too started that way but, as a trainer and a competitive handler, I can tell you that Open competition today is not what it was ten or fifteen or more years ago. For one thing, the size of the classes has grown immensely, to the point that seventy runs in an Open class is not uncommon, whereas when I started trialing I was competing against perhaps ten or fifteen handlers. Another aspect to consider is the improvement in the technical ability of today's

♠ FROM THE HANDLER'S POST ♠

handlers. There are more careful breeding programs in the United States today, more trainers, more opportunities to practice competitive handling, and all of these factors have contributed to make Open-level competition much more difficult than it was a decade or two ago.

When I started out, and this was the case for many handlers at that time, the winning Open run might be one where the sheep had missed an entire panel; today, a run needs to be nearly perfect to win. Handlers therefore need a trialing system that, like a good training program, allows them to advance step by step, to get the mileage they need, and to improve while building a solid foundation.

In some cases, due to the increased size of Open classes, trials have adopted a standard, whereby any run which is not in the "competitive" category (that is, any run in which so many points have already been lost that it would not be able to place in the top twenty percent of the class) is terminated by the judge before it is completed. This is not something that any of us like to see, but many of us have had to utilize this system or run under it in order to allow everyone a chance to compete. Often, a beginning Open handler is called off under this standard and does not get the chance to complete his run. Perhaps part of the opposition stems from the term "Open Ranch," which does not really describe the class at all. A more accurate description of the class's intended function would be "Advanced Pro-Novice" or "Started Open," which would clarify to all handlers how this class fits in with the others. It would have a full drive, but might have a shorter outrun than in the Open class.

Finally, the addition of this "Advanced Pro-Novice/Ranch" class would have benefits for the Pro-Novice class as well. Pro-Novice handlers would not have to compete in a field of Open handlers and their dogs. I have attended many trials recently where the same dogs continue to compete at the Pro-Novice level, threatening to become "professional Pro-Novice dogs," because their handlers know that they are not ready to compete at the Open level. Some of these dogs have been Open dogs under different handlers, but these newer handlers have not acquired the mileage to move up themselves. These dogs and handlers really should not drop down to Pro-Novice, but they should be running in a more advanced class level. Also, if the Advanced Pro-Novice/Ranch class is in place, Pro-Novice handlers would have a better idea of what type of course to expect when they travel to a trial. Currently, they might face anything from a just-above-Novice course to a just-below-Open course. The four-tier system would allow han-

♠ FROM THE HANDLER'S POST ♠

dlers to progress at increasingly difficult levels until finally moving to the Open level. Adding this class costs nothing and caught on quickly in the regions where it has become the rule.

The Open Class in Stockdog Trials

When you and your dog feel ready to move up one more notch, we are talking Open. This is the top level of competition that is offered in the trial system.

The Open class offers the highest degree of difficulty in terms of the technical skill and the ability to "read" sheep/stock of dog and handler. Before you plan to move up to Open, it is important to realize/evaluate just what you and your dog are actually able to do in a very controlled way. For instance, your dog needs to be able to do an outrun of a minimum of 350 yards. Your dog should be able to drive a course of at least a total of 400 yards with a high degree of accuracy. You both need to be accomplished at penning. And, then there is the shed! Sometimes a split may be asked for or it might be a single. Expecting or hoping that luck will play a part is less than reliable. It takes a lot of time and skill on the part of both you and your dog to learn the art of shedding. When you feel confident that you and your dog can accomplish these areas of work, then take a deep breath and move up!

There are two schools of thought on how to run the Open class: most believe in the current system of one class where all Open handlers, regardless of experience, run together—from a handler in Open for the first time to those that have competed at this level for twenty, thirty, or more years. There are some however, who believe that the Open class should consist of two levels, the first for those recently moved into Open and the second for longtime Open handlers, including the so-called professionals.

There is a standard course for Open consisting of the "outwork" (outrun, lift and fetch); a drive of three legs with two sets of drive panels, one as the transition from the first to the second leg of the drive, and the second as the transition from the second to the third leg of the drive. The drive is usually in the shape of a triangle. The sheep are then brought to either the pen or the shedding ring. The pen may complete the course when it follows the shed; however, it may also precede the shed. At some trials, the pen follows the shed, and then a second shed, typically a single, is performed. Fortunately, there is room for "free thinking" in the overall setting of an Open course, allowing the course to accommodate natural obstacles such as a clump of trees that require a dog-leg

♠ FROM THE HANDLER'S POST ♠

fetch, or a bridge that is incorporated into a drive; hopefully, this freedom will never change. That being said, artificially-created difficulties that require more luck than skill should be carefully considered before being added to a course. The tremendous number of variables provided by nature, landscape, and the sheep that confront an Open handler create enough of a challenge ensuring excitement for handler, dog, and spectator alike.

Good luck and good running!

3

The Outrun

From a position near to the handler who stands at the post, the dog should run out, either right or left, in a cast which is neither too straight nor too wide, arriving behind his sheep at sufficient distance from them not to unduly disturb them.
—20 points

Anticipation is the difference between a glitch and a disaster. With a young dog, the difference between his level of control at home and at the trial field may be as much as 50%; in other words, a difficulty that might be reparable at home results in an out-of-control situation on the trial field. And in terms of spotting the sheep, the terrain and the type of sheep might be different from those that the dog is accustomed to, so the set-up for the outrun becomes much more crucial.

Young dogs are often caught off-guard by sheep that are more difficult to see, or a flat field instead of the hills he is used to, or sometimes a distance that is a little longer than he has been practicing. If the trial is running quickly or the set-out point is close to the holding pen, the sheep might already be in place by the time you and your dog reach the post, so that the dog does not have the sheep's movement as an aid. Your training program and your on-site homework must include preparing your dog and yourself for these eventualities.

One step that should always be taken at trials, particularly with young dogs, is to bring them up to the fence at the beginning of a run, once or twice prior to their run, so that they can spot the sheep at the top of the field. You should take the dog to the fence, tell him to "look" as the sheep are brought out or as the other dog is doing his outrun, and watch your dog's head and eyes so that you are certain that he does see the sheep. Let him watch the outrun, lift, and first half of the fetch; then praise the dog and walk away from the fence,

♠ FROM THE HANDLER'S POST ♠

out of sight of the field. Remember that you don't need for your dog to see another handler's potential wreck, for example if the sheep should run toward the exhaust pen. Very often, handlers with young dogs will sit under the tent or in the spectator area and let their dogs watch sheep be exhausted from the field during run after run. I see this happen at many trials: the handler is socializing but the dog is studying the field. This obviously creates the possibility that your dog will run to the exhaust pen rather than to the set-out sheep. This is an easily avoidable danger, and inexperienced handlers really need to be alert that they are not creating a potential problem.

The above suggestions are part of the "homework" that you should do at the trial, before your run. Of course, if you are first in the running order, you lose the possibility of many of these homework steps. But if you do have time, it is to your advantage to study and prepare, rather than socializing or fussing with your dog, so that you are ready for potential problems. Some handlers claim that it helps, before your run, to visualize the perfect run. This may be true for them, but I think that there is more to gain from visualizing all of the potential problems and mapping out your strategy for handling them in such a way that you are a help to your dog.

Other homework tips include studying the terrain and the pressures and considering how they will affect your particular dog. In other words, a ridge or a ditch that is not a problem to tight-running dogs may be disastrous for wider-running dogs. This should influence your decision about which way to send your dog, so that he loses sight of the sheep as little as possible. You should not just imitate what the handlers before you do, because every dog is an individual, and you are the one who best knows your dog's working style and habits.

Another preparatory step that will help your dog spot the sheep consistently involves your approach to the handler's post. You should imagine that the fetch line continues well beyond the post itself. Then, as you enter the gate, you should place yourself and your dog on that line, with the dog close by your side; walk toward the post at such an angle that the set-out spot is at twelve o'clock. This is particularly important at trials where the sheep are not set out in the center of the field. Your dog should know that the sheep are somewhere directly in front of the line you are walking, on your approach. In this way, even if he does not find the sheep, he will trust you and his outrun will follow the correct path, reducing the chance of a crossover while he is looking for them. This also reduces the chance that the exhaust pen,

♠ FROM THE HANDLER'S POST ♠

which may not be well hidden at some trials, will distract him. The dog who is comfortable with a set-up routine will always be looking up the field for his sheep, and not off to your side or behind you.

Your entrance to the field and your approach to the post should take place as early as possible, just as soon as the previous sheep are out of sight. This increases the chances that your dog will be able to watch the sheep on their way from the holding area to the set-out spot, when they are easier to spot. One aid that you can use here is the truck or trailer in which the judge is sitting. This vehicle is generally located directly on line; you and your dog can stand near it in such a way that it blocks the dog's view of the exhaust, and thus you do not have to wait until the previous sheep are completely put away before you start your dog looking up the field.

Movement is the best key to help your dog find the sheep before you send him. Some handlers complain when the sheep are not completely settled, but often this can be an aid to you, because it draws your dog's attention to the correct spot. Of course, you should then allow the sheep to settle as much as possible before sending your dog.

Walk part of the way to the post, and then stop and allow your dog to set up on the sheep. It is important that you not walk all the way to the post, because your dog may be keyed up and may try to leave your side early; if you call him back to you at the post, you will lose almost all of your outrun points. However, if you need to call him back during the approach, while you are well behind the post, you do not lose any points at all. I advocate that you do not proceed to the post itself until the sheep are settled and you are quite certain that your dog sees them.

    Although you should be looking primarily up field (so that your dog follows your line of vision), you should also be watching your dog peripherally, to be aware of potential problems. The dog should not need to be on a leash during this approach; if you cannot control your dog during a set-up, this indicates 1) that you have not developed a consistent routine during your training program, and 2) that there is a good chance you will have greater problems during your run than this one! It is important that your dog be somewhat calm and focused, and that you control your own nerves. Don't rush yourself or your dog. If necessary, remind yourself not to worry about hurrying, or about what the judge is thinking. The clock does not start until you send your dog, and a few extra seconds here can save your entire run.

♠ FROM THE HANDLER'S POST ♠

After you have set up the dog, take one more second to make certain that the dog is not looking across you; in other words, looking to your left when he is set up on your right, or vice versa. Body angle is also indicative of potential crossovers. This often happens because the dog has spotted something else that he thinks are the sheep (for example, large rocks, stumps, feeders). It may be impossible for you to convince your dog that those are not the sheep. In such a case, your best course of action is to prevent the dog from crossing over by sending him toward the side he is looking. As he approaches the objects, you hope that he will realize that they are not sheep in time to look up field and correct his own approach.

In such a situation, your trial strategy must include avoiding a crossover. At many trials, it is quite apparent to me that the dog is about to cross at the handler's feet (resulting in a deduction of eighteen or nineteen of the twenty outrun points), but it catches the handler by surprise. If you feel that the dog might cross over, then back up from the post and re-do your set-up routine, with the dog farther out to your side. If you cannot correct this, then you should consider sending your dog the other way. I am not in any way an advocate of allowing the dog to choose his direction for the outrun, because the handler needs to consider many factors and make this decision wisely. However, with a young dog that seems to be insisting on a crossover because he is not fixed on the sheep, it may be safer for you to yield and send him from the other side.

Your care and consistency in the above steps will help you to avoid the problem of the dog not spotting the sheep. However, it may happen that the dog seems to see the sheep, and you send him, only to realize that he is scanning the field or cutting in early, or running to the holding area at the top of the field. In these cases, you need to make sure that both you and your dog have the necessary tools to prevent this from being irreparable, as we shall discuss in the next section.

After you have taken all of the necessary steps to maximize the chances that your dog will see the sheep before you send him, you will still need to have in mind your strategy for helping him in case it starts to fall apart after you have sent him. He may leave your feet with apparent certainty, but early in the outrun you can see him scanning the field, looking for sheep, perhaps cutting in from the ideal pear-shaped outrun path.

In such a case, it is *fundamental* for you to remember that, in the Novice and Pro-Novice classes, the objective is not to win the trial, but rather to use this trial as training for the next

♠ FROM THE HANDLER'S POST ♠

trial and as a positive learning experience. Therefore, the very instant that your dog starts to cut in early, you must forget about points, and not remain silently hoping for the best, hoping for self-correction. The few points you would lose for a well-timed command are nothing compared to the possibility of a crossover or of the dog not finding the sheep at all.

As soon as the dog starts to cut in, I recommend that you hit him with a strong "stop" whistle or command. Even though it involves a lesser loss of points, a running re-direct is often not effective with inexperienced dogs—once they have chosen a path they are often committed to it. A young dog is also not likely to correct his own outrun path by kicking out when he spots the sheep; he is much more likely to head straight for them in his relief at having found sheep at last! So get your dog off his feet, giving him and you time to think through the situation. Don't hope for the best; instead, create your own luck.

If the dog is not certain of the location of the sheep, then as soon as you lie him down you will see him looking anxiously for the sheep, or looking back to you for help. He may actually spot the sheep during this moment. Then you should give a "get out" or a flank command; but if the dog's *very first* steps are not correct, stop him again; do not allow him to cross over or to head directly toward the sheep. I would reiterate that you must eliminate all thought of "points" at this time and make sure that your dog is correct; you can only lose twenty points here, and you may save the remainder of your run, through clear thinking and preparedness.

Part of your preparation at the trial should have included asking the judge, at the handler's meeting, what you are allowed to do if the dog has difficulty in finding the sheep. Most judges will—and really should—allow you to walk upfield toward the sheep and help your dog. If so, and if your dog runs into trouble, do not hesitate to do this, even though it may signal the end of your run. This is much better than the alternative of frustrating and confusing your dog with shouts of "look back" and inappropriate flank commands. Keep the dog stopped and get in a position to help him learn from the experience. This is also a useful strategy at a two-day trial, because it will reduce the chances of the same thing happening the next day.

It is generally not helpful to call the dog all the way back to you and re-send; often he will repeat the same error. Instead, you should handle the situation to the dog's best advantage, and then afterward mentally review your training program. If there are no holes in the foundation of your training, then 1) you will be able to stop the dog fairly easily during the

♠ FROM THE HANDLER'S POST ♠

outrun, and 2) the subsequent command will kick him out and further up the field. If you watch the advanced classes at trials, you will see that even though those dogs also sometimes do not find their sheep. It does not signal the end of their run, but rather is a correctable situation. The next section will discuss how your at-home training can prepare you and your dog to handle these situations, when they do happen.

You may need to help the dog if the outrun path means that he will lose sight of the sheep, through a combination of tricky terrain and a natural wide outrun. My recommendation in this case is that, once he disappears, you gauge his speed and path and blow a stop whistle when you estimate that he is at about eleven o'clock, so that he stops somewhere near twelve o'clock. Then, rather than give a walk-up whistle, I would give a recall whistle, particularly with younger dogs. A walk-up whistle doesn't make much sense to a dog that still is not in sight of the sheep. Often, it will make him continue on his outrun path, because the dog doesn't know what else to do. A recall whistle, hopefully, will bring the dog into view. As soon as you can see that the dog sees the sheep, then stop the dog again and give your walk-in whistle. As we discussed earlier, with young dogs you should not remain silent and hope for the best; you should be an active participant and help your dog to find the sheep with a minimum of confusion or frustration.

One factor that keeps some dogs from finding their sheep is that they become fixed on the sheep in the exhaust pen. Careful homework can prevent this from being an insurmountable problem. First, even in the early stages you should be teaching some form of a "look back" command, which teaches the dog to take his attention off the sheep he is working and look for a different group. This command is most easily taught by having the dog split a large flock of sheep, wear one group a short distance away, and then turn back to bring the other group. In addition to teaching the command itself, this trains your dog to break his concentration on the flock he is working, which in itself is a very valuable and useful skill.

Your homework should also make sure that your dog has a set-up routine, that he understands not to fetch any group of sheep that is off to your side or behind you. He should always bring the group of sheep that you are facing. Sheep in adjacent pens or other areas of the field are simply off-limits. As you train, you should not endeavor to eliminate all possible distractions, but rather you should teach your dog to deal with those distractions.

♠ FROM THE HANDLER'S POST ♠

For example, work a group of sheep while another small group is standing nearby, sometimes in a fenced-off area and sometimes out in the same field. You can split the sheep, take one group away to a safe distance (where they will not immediately run back to the other group), and then walk away with your dog. You should then set your dog up on the one group that he has been working, and have him bring them, teaching him to leave the other group undisturbed. In the early stages, you should always send the young dog to the outside rather than between the two flocks; as he comes around the back of the group you want him to bring, you may need to whistle him in so that he does not continue and gather the entire flock. As the training progresses, you can teach him to go between the two flocks, if they are separated by enough distance. (Of course, at other times you should let him know to gather both groups, so that he does not lose the ability to group and bring in a spread-out flock. What you are teaching here, in your various exercises, is flexibility, adaptability, teaching the dog to do what you need done in a given situation.)

Another way to refine this ability to work separate groups of sheep is to begin as above, splitting the sheep and wearing one group away from the other. Then, have the dog push the group past you, and behind you. Finally, call him back to your side and set him up on the remaining group. To do this, he will have to forget about those sheep which are behind you, and he will learn that his sheep are the ones out in front.

You can teach your dog a great deal about fences during your training, and this work will help if he gets fixed on the sheep in the exhaust or holding pens. Here, those who train on larger farms have a distinct advantage. If you only have one field and one small flock, then you must gain this experience by visiting larger farms or training areas. The dog must learn that sheep that are on the opposite side of the fence are *not his sheep*. He should not try to go under the fence, or run up and down the fence trying to bring those sheep; rather, he should turn away and look for sheep in the field where you are. One exercise is to have a group of sheep on the fence in an adjacent pen or field, and have another group of sheep on your side of the fence but right next to the others. Then send your dog. He will first think that he can go around the entire flock, but soon he will realize that the only sheep he is to worry about are those on his side of the fence. This will prepare him for the eventuality that, in a trial, the set-out sheep break back to the holding pen

♠ FROM THE HANDLER'S POST ♠

or to the exhaust, so that you can salvage your run.

Another training exercise that will enhance your dog's ability to spot the correct sheep is to have someone holding sheep for you. This person should hold a small group of sheep; you will approach your "post" and send the dog, bring the sheep, and put them in a pen or field behind you; then immediately have the holder bring another group, and send the dog for them. Repeat this exercise six or eight times, so that the dog learns that the sheep upfield, or those toward which you are walking, are the ones he is supposed to work, and he will not worry about the sheep behind him. When you see some Open handlers dare to walk onto the field even before the previous sheep are off the field, you can be sure that their dogs are prepared and have enough mileage to know that those sheep being exhausted are not theirs. They will already be looking up the field for their group.

Finally, in order to have the necessary tools to help your dog during a trial, you must be able to stop your dog during the outrun. Often, inexperienced handlers who train dogs that outrun quite naturally have never needed to stop the dog at the midpoint of the outrun—or even later—and they assume that they could do so if necessary. But even a dog that has a good lie-down may forget all about that once he is sent on an outrun, or he may become accustomed to not stopping from the time he leaves your feet until he reaches the sheep. You should practice stopping the dog once in a while, even during a correct outrun, as part of your training program. Even if he looks like he is out wide enough, if you tell him to do so, he should kick out wider, trusting you rather than following his own instincts. This level of control most certainly will come in handy in some unforeseen trial situation. So use this as one of your "yardsticks" for measuring the degree of teamwork you are developing with your dog. You should not overdo this exercise to the degree that you make your dog hesitant. However, you should be able to stop and re-direct the dog any time you need. He should be listening *all* the time, in case you need to correct some assumption or intention on his part.

All of these training exercises will make the difference between a problem that causes a loss of a few points, and a problem that costs you your entire run. When I hear a handler blame the dog or the terrain for his not finding the sheep, I know also that the handler either did not prepare the right tools ahead of time for assisting the dog in such an eventuality, or else did not use those tools appropriately when the dog got confused. One last point: when you hear a handler tell a story like "My run fell

♠ FROM THE HANDLER'S POST ♠

apart because the dog didn't find the sheep," never assume that this could not happen to you. Think about your own training, and about what you are equipped to do when—not if—your dog has trouble finding the sheep at some future trial.

As we discussed, the most certain prevention of the crossover problem also has to do with setting your dog up at the post. He should be set up a short distance away from you, with his body turned slightly outward and his head looking toward the sheep. Many crossovers happen right at your feet, and this results in a loss of nineteen points right from the start; as a spectator I can often predict these crossovers, when I see that the dog is looking directly across the field in front of the handler, and/or is set up too close to the handler's leg. It is very important that you as a handler take a moment to anticipate this problem.

Additionally, it is very important that you approach the post in a straight line that points directly toward the sheep. Often the handlers' entrance gate is not directly on that line, the imaginary line from the sheep to the post. In such a case, you should enter the gate, and then follow the fence line or stay well behind the post until you and your dog are on that imaginary line. Then begin your approach to the post, making sure to watch your dog; if he is looking across the field, stop and correct this before reaching the post itself. This reduces the probability of a "false start," and allows you the rest of the approach time to fix in your dog's mind the path he should follow on the outrun. I cannot stress enough the importance of not rushing the approach to the post, in spite of your own nervousness and the pressure of "post etiquette." Of course, trial organizers hope that there will not be substantial delays in the trial, but you and your dog deserve the chance to perform to the best of your ability and to demonstrate the results of your careful training program. This can all fall apart quickly if you rush your young dog and result in a crossover.

All of this post work ends when the dog leaves your feet, and then the terrain of the field takes over in influencing the path of the outrun. Other factors that come into play here are the similarity or difference between the trial field and your usual training field, and also whether you have been able to practice with your dog on several varied fields and terrains. An ideal training program, as we have discussed, includes not only trialing on different fields, but also training on different fields, where you can teach your dog to adjust to any terrain, to the unfamiliar or the unexpected, or to re-direction commands from you, if necessary. Aspects of the terrain which should alert you to the possi-

♠ FROM THE HANDLER'S POST ♠

bility of a crossover include a hill, a valley, or an old path, road, or fence line across the course. We all have said, and have heard others say, "My dog never does this at home." All that indicates to me is that this dog is uncomfortable or lost when he is away from home, and the dog needs to be trained away from home more often. Study the terrain, anticipate the possibility of a crossover, and correct firmly at the instant that it begins to happen.

In addition to the variation of terrain, dogs also need to adjust to variation in the length of the outrun. Many people train on outruns that are about two-thirds of the length of an actual trial outrun, thus unconsciously teaching their dog to come in at the same point every time rather than adjusting to the position of the sheep. Your training program should also include surprisingly long outruns for your dog, outruns that are as much as twice as long as those in a trial. After a false start or two, your dog will learn to keep running, keep widening out, until he is in fact beyond the sheep, before starting to cut in.

No training program is foolproof, however, and careful observation and quick reactions are the key to stopping an imminent crossover. "My dog crossed over" really means "I didn't (or couldn't) stop my dog before he reached the fetch line." The very second that the dog starts to tip in toward the fetch line, hit the brakes! Particularly with young dogs, a "running redirect" will only speed the dog up on his current course. A stop, on the other hand, gives the dog time to think, to focus in on your command; then you should give a wide flank command. If the dog does not kick out immediately, stop him again. Do not wait and hope that he sees the sheep and kicks out on his own, because in a trial you need to make your own luck, by careful timing and anticipation. Also, it is crucial that you do not think about the judge, about loss of points, or about maximizing your score. Rather, you should think of this trial primarily as practice for the next trial: stop your dog and leave the post if necessary, rather than allowing a crossover and hoping for the best.

If the dog does cross over but then kicks wide off the sheep, recovering his composure for the lift and fetch, then a crossover should not cause your entire run to fall apart. Often, however, a young dog or even an older dog will panic or get confused when he realizes that he is crossing between you and the sheep; he will ring the sheep at the top or come in too close, hit them hard on the lift, chase them during the fetch, and then it is true that the crossover ruined your run. It may even be that the crossover was just one symptom that the dog was nervous and out of control in the first place.

♠ FROM THE HANDLER'S POST ♠

However, after the crossover, the subsequent chain of events can sometimes be avoided. Both you and the dog need to recover your composure; the best way to do this is with a full stop. Lie the dog down, think a moment, let the dog think a moment—not too long, of course, if the sheep have already begun to run—and then give a flank or walk-up command which will bring your dog back under control, or get him listening to you instead of working on his own.

In terms of the earlier training, the best way to reduce the probability of crossovers is not to stretch the dog out too early, when he is learning the outrun. It is much better to spend weeks perfecting a wide, smooth outrun than to measure distance and put pressure on yourself and the dog. Short, correct outruns should become an absolute habit for the dog; the dog must learn to gauge his distance off the sheep on his own, and automatically. If this foundation is properly laid, and if the dog is in fact thinking on his own, then it will not take long at all to stretch out the length—when the time is right. Then your chances of success at those early trials are really maximized. Be patient, and don't rush your dog!

4

The Lift

Whether the dog has stopped or slowed down his approach should be smooth and steady and he should take control of his sheep in a quiet, firm manner.
— 10 points

If your packet of sheep get away early before or as your dog reaches the top of the outrun, you should realize first that it may not always be a reflection of the spotter's abilities. The spotter has a tremendous responsibility for holding things together during the outrun and lift, there is no doubt about that. How he holds the sheep, and how he sets them up, can make or break a run. However, he is working with animals, and you are working with animals, and so there are many variables at work each time you go to the post and the spotter heads out with his dog(s) and group of sheep. Unexpected things are going to happen.

You cannot let your run fall apart just because something goes wrong at the top; your job as a handler is to put things back together, to hold your dog—and yourself—together, to stabilize the situation and move on to the next phase of your run. You cannot make excuses as soon as the problem happens, and walk off the field; instead, you have to continue your run and let the *judge* decide how to handle the problem at the top. The judge may indeed decide that your run was ruined by that problem, and then he or she will call you off the field; but that is the judge's decision, by which you agreed to abide when you entered the field. So don't exacerbate the problem by waiting with your head cocked, allowing a chase or an off-line fetch to continue, listening for the judge to give you a re-run. Instead, get to work and put your run back together.

Most likely, the judge will not call you off, but rather will adjust the points so that you are not unduly penalized, if he or she is certain that you did not cause or contribute to the problem. You will receive your ten lift points, which might be more than you would otherwise have earned, and the fetch line will be gauged differently. In such a case, you need to be sure not to lose

♠ FROM THE HANDLER'S POST ♠

your concentration, and not to allow your dog to lose concentration. Gain control of the situation so that the rest of your run is not adversely affected by the events of the first few seconds.

When the lift happens in an unexpected way, you need to read the sheep as quickly and accurately as you can; you will need to flank your dog quickly to straighten out the line and to have your dog covering the sheep—of course, the better dogs will help here by flanking on their own and thus help the recovery.

If the lift falls apart, a young dog may lose his head easily. The very best insurance you have against this is to get the dog off his feet *immediately*. As soon as the problem begins, whistle a hard "lie down" and then warn him to "stay out" before flanking him. This gives both you and the dog a second or two to collect yourselves. It also allows for a wider flank with the young dog, for three reasons: 1) he is under your command instead of chasing sheep; 2) his forward momentum has been stopped, so he is less likely to slice the angle of the flank; and 3) the distance between him and the sheep has increased somewhat, thus releasing pressure and making it easier for him to widen out.

If the dog has a tendency to blow into the sheep or panic in this type of situation, maintain a strong hold on him during these seconds; you may want to stop him again after the flank, just to make sure that you and he stay in constant contact. Here, the important thing is that you know your dog well, and anticipate his probable reactions. If this kind of situation causes him to go into a "chase mode" at home, then you can bet it will have an even greater effect on the trial field; don't just hope for the best, make the best happen.

You need to act in advance of the dog's movements, rather than waiting and reacting. Of course, all of this happens within a few seconds—either you recover or you lose control of the situation—but careful anticipation can help you be ready for this situation. As I have said before, a lot can be gained by your mental preparation. Don't think about the perfect run, because those are few and far between. Rather, think about the "what ifs," and about what you will do if this or that unfortunate situation occurs. This is how you will develop "handler strategies" that will keep you from having to explain why your run fell apart. You may lose some points, but it will not cost you your entire run.

Of course, you cannot be too specific and analytical about this; Situation A does not always require Response B. Rather, your strategy needs to be to react appropriately, given the specifics of the event that occurred and the dog

♠ FROM THE HANDLER'S POST ♠

that you are running. Your knowledge of what will be appropriate comes only from mileage, from setting up similar situations at home. If you have practiced often with a spotter holding the sheep, then it is likely that that spotter has let the sheep go, or moved at the wrong time, thus inadvertently creating practice "opportunities" for you and your dog. If you keep your mind active during your practice sessions and take advantage of bad situations in order to learn something and teach your dog something, then you will be a better handler on the trial field, and be ready for all eventualities.

Many trials do try to even the playing field or steady the sheep by holding them with corn, rather than using a single spotter throughout the day. I understand why people do this, so that all of the handlers presumably have an equal chance of the sheep staying in place. However, I do not advocate this as it can create difficulties, and makes for unequal lifts and makes fair judging very difficult. There are two reasons that holding with corn creates difficulties: one is that the sheep are often less alert to the dog's approach, and thus they tend to bolt when they realize that the dog is suddenly behind them. The other is that your dog has become used to the sheep's heads coming up, their ears moving or flicking as they prepare to start moving when they are not held on corn, and your dog has learned to use these cues to read pressure and to modulate his lift accordingly. If the sheep are eating corn, all of their heads are down, and your dog is suddenly confused at the sheep's lack of reaction to his approach. He may stop short, or overrun, or lift harder than he normally does. Again, the best cure is an ounce of prevention. If you know that they will use corn at the trial, then you should use corn in your practice the week before.

You should be ready to help your dog at the top, more than you would need to do if there were no corn. Be ready to push the dog on if he stops early; be ready to stop him if he starts to overrun; or be ready to stop him if he lifts too hard. Ideally, if the sheep do not see your dog at the top, you should stop your dog, and then flank a little one way or the other, until one of the sheep notices him and signals to the others. This will reduce your chances that they bolt away; it may cost you a point or two, with some judges, but it may save you the several points that you would lose on an off-line fetch, or the whole run if you allowed a chase or a grip to result.

As regards the holding of the sheep, there are several things that it is helpful for a competitor to know, during the week of tune-up before a trial. Here is a list of some questions that you can contact the trial organizers to find

♠ FROM THE HANDLER'S POST ♠

out, in order to enhance your own preparedness:

- What kind of sheep will be used?
- How will the sheep will be held?
- How long will the outrun be for each class?
- What is the terrain of the field?

I recommend that, if you are serious about trialing, you create the habit of finding out this information and adjusting your practice accordingly.

This has been a detailed description of what happens in a very few seconds. However, those moments of initial contact between the dog and sheep, and between you and your dog, have a great deal to do with the rest of your run. The point I most want to stress, with the problems we have discussed and with all trialing situations, is the importance of preparedness, in both your training program and your handling strategies. By doing your homework in three areas—on the practice field, finding out key information before the trial, and watching prior runs—you can reduce by 80% the chances of having to make excuses later about why you and your dog were unsuccessful. You do not need to win or place at every trial, but you do need to leave the field feeling good about what you and your dog were able to accomplish together, and this means anticipating the glitches that can turn into disasters, and having the control over yourself and your dog to put things back together and recover from the mistakes, whether they are the spotter's, your dog's, or yours.

In your training program, when you first start working a dog with a spotter, you really do need a good, experienced person holding the sheep, and this person needs to have firm control over his or her dog. In this early phase of training, chaos at the top of the outrun can really create problems or bad habits. But as the training continues and your dog builds confidence, you need to build flexibility into your dog. So have your spotter move around as the dog reaches the top of the outrun; have the spotter lie his dog down directly in front of the sheep, so that your dog has to push sheep over the top of him; have the spotter wave a stick or speak to his own dog, but be alert to encourage your dog and walk him in, so that your dog learns to ignore such distractions.

Don't practice for the perfect situation, but rather practice for the potential pitfalls. At home, you can decrease the length of the outrun when you practice these sorts of problems, in order to hold things together. You can have the spotter be more subtle in his movements or

♠ FROM THE HANDLER'S POST ♠

actions. Then increase the distance, or the spotter's distractions, so that you are teaching your dog to adjust to whatever happens, and to keep his attention focused on you and your commands *no matter what*. Additionally, having the spotter place his dog right in front of the sheep can really help you teach your dog how to do a proper lift; this slows down the action, and allows you to assert your control over the situation.

Now that we have discussed the training problems, and the ways to minimize the consequences, we can talk about specific handler strategies. One hint I repeat often is the importance of watching the runs prior to your own. You should study the demeanor of the sheep and also the techniques of the spotters, to see whether they are letting the sheep go early, moving a little too much, placing their dog in front of the sheep—which is sometimes necessary with flighty sheep—or what you can expect when your dog gets to the top. This also gives you a chance to study the pressures, so that you are ready with a quick flank, or to stop your dog early, if the situation should require that.

If the sheep do leave early, then you should realize that you will probably not be penalized by a loss of lift points. However, often the sheep do not head straight down the fetch line when they leave early. In this case, if you do not have your dog in position to gain control and put the sheep on line, you may indeed lose points. You may clarify specific judging policies during the handlers' meeting, but the general rule used by most judges is that, if the sheep leave the spotter early, the fetch line will begin from wherever you pick up the sheep, and goes from that point *directly* to the center of the fetch gates, and then straight to the post from there. This is only true if the sheep leave on their own or because of the spotter; the rules are different if your dog sliced the outrun or lifted wrong and therefore pushed the sheep off-line.

It often happens that spotters need to put their dogs directly in front of the sheep to hold them for you. This can really be to your advantage, because it allows you time to lie your dog down and gain control, without the sheep running away. But then you need to be ready, in case spotters cannot call their dogs out of the way; your dog needs to lie down, and you wait to see if the spotter does pull his/her dog aside. But if the spotter does not do that, then have your dog walk up slowly and steadily, and then *stop* at the instant that you see the first movements of the sheep. Let the sheep find their own way around the spotter's dog, rather than having your dog push them into the other dog. By using this strategy, you can minimize

♠ FROM THE HANDLER'S POST ♠

panic or jumping on the part of the sheep. After they are past the spotter's dog, then walk your dog up, put the sheep back on line (be alert and ready with a quick flank if necessary), and then continue your fetch.

Now, if the problem is that the spotter moved, or spoke, or waved a stick and it startled your dog, then the important thing is that you encourage your dog to come back to the sheep. Here again it is fundamental that you have your homework done. Handlers, particularly newer handlers, need to realize that this is not the time to train your dog. You cannot train your dog on the trial field. If you know that your dog is sensitive to the spotter's movements, then you need already to have decided whether you can get the dog through these situations, or whether perhaps that dog does not have the temperament for competitive trialing. The only way to assess your dog's potential, and the ways for you best to help that dog, is to work out the situation at home, beforehand, and know how to employ the best teamwork possible.

Again, it is important to train flexibility into your dog, in informal situations where you can control the outcomes to a greater degree than you can at a trial. Don't train always with the same spotter, who becomes familiar to the dog. Have strangers hold, vary between men and women, go to different fields, use different sheep. All of these training initiatives will allow your dog to mature and to adjust to whatever unexpected situations might arise. Train your dog to be adaptable, and to take things in stride.

5

The Fetch

Once the sheep are on the move (lifted) they should be brought at a steady pace through the gates to the handler. The fetch ends when the sheep have been passed around behind the handler and then the drive begins.
– 20 points

Handlers ask many questions about situations that occurred during the fetch portion of the trial—questions having to do with the reaction of the sheep, the dog being out of control or not flanking correctly, or with a loss of points that seems unreasonable to the handler. Many of these questions can be answered by a discussion of the two most important aspects of the fetch—accuracy (in terms of the "fetch line") and pace.

Remember that 99% of the time, the judge is sitting on the fetch line; the judge knows exactly where that fetch line is, and the handler had best know as well. This means examining the line well in advance of your own run and being aware of its location not only when you get to the fetch panels (if there are panels), but all the way from the set-out to your feet. ANY deviation from that straight line involves a potential loss of points.

It helps some handlers to stand behind the handler's post (unless of course the post is too tall!), so that they can sight a line between the post and the center of the fetch gates. It is also best to choose a landmark directly on the fetch line, behind the set-out spot—a fence post, tree, etc. This will help you maintain your fix on the line once the spotter and dog have moved away from the set-out location. Remember that the judge has probably already done this and is judging you accordingly, so it behooves you to do the same.

Two possible variations on the fetch line should be understood. If the sheep are not set out directly on-line, if and only if you are certain that your dog is not responsible for the sheep starting out off-line, then you may assume that the fetch line is directly from that set-out point to the center of the fetch panels, and then from the center of the fetch panels to

♠ FROM THE HANDLER'S POST ♠

your feet. (If you are in any doubt about this rule, then ask the judge at the handler's meeting, but this is pretty much a general rule, and if the judge does not feel that way, he probably will tell you so.) And if there are no fetch panels, then the line is directly from where the sheep are lifted to your feet.

When sheep are very light, it may be difficult for the spotter to select the exact spot, and it is in fact to your advantage to take the sheep when they are calm and settled, rather than trying to demand that the spotter make that small adjustment for you. It is likely that your sheep will be less spooked and you will have a better fetch score, provided that you understand how to react accordingly, and provided that you have the requisite control of your dog to negotiate that "dog-leg-style" fetch line.

The other variation occurs when the sheep start out off-line because your dog has chopped the top of the outrun or lifted incorrectly. In this case, your best option in terms of points is to take the sheep directly back to the fetch line—a 90-degree turn if necessary—and then resume the fetch on-line. This is often difficult, because if the dog chopped the top of the outrun he has already spooked the sheep. But in such a case, you must make the best of it, get the dog under control, get the sheep turned, and resume your fetch.

In both cases, some handlers find that they and their dogs do not have the necessary tools in their possession to get this job done. They might practice on-line fetches all the time at home and feel that the dog is well under control during the fetch, because he takes flank commands as they are given. But if all of these practice flank commands are given to maintain balance, to keep the sheep coming directly toward you, then you are not building the necessary flexibility into your dog to be able to handle unexpected situations. Your dog may be working more on his own than you realize. The dog has become habituated to bringing the sheep directly to you, so that when more precision is required (i.e. a dog-leg fetch or a sharp turn to return to the fetch line), the dog refuses the flank command, and you miss the panels, or he slices that flank because he is uncomfortable with it, or the sheep in fact do come to you but never have been on the fetch line at all. Any of these situations will result in a significant loss of points.

You should use the following barometer in your training program at home to see whether your dog is working on your instruction or is primarily working on his own: as the dog is bringing the sheep to you, flank him all the way around to the front of the sheep, so that the sheep make a 180-degree turn, then have the

♠ FROM THE HANDLER'S POST ♠

dog push the sheep directly back in the direction they came from. Many of you will find, to your surprise, that your dog will not do this if this is the first time you are trying it. The dog is used to flanking for balance—moving between the 9:00 and the 3:00 spot on the clock face. When you ask for more than that, you are asking that the dog drop his own natural instincts in order to follow your instructions. While we all want our dogs to develop and use their "natural" instincts, it is an absolute requirement for trialing that, when necessary, the dog subordinate these instincts to your instructions. Turning the sheep 90 degrees to go back to the fetch line is a learned skill that is based on handler-dog teamwork, not on natural instinct.

After you have flanked your dog 180 degrees during this practice fetch, flank him back around to resume the fetch, and then immediately flank 180 degrees in the *other* direction. Drive the sheep away from you a little more, then flank the dog back around to balance and continue the fetch. This exercise should be done periodically in order to *anticipate* and *prepare for* the unexpected trial situation. You will then have this weapon in your arsenal, not *in case* you ever need it, but *when* you need it. It is only a matter of time before this situation will happen to you, either because of the terrain and the sheep or because of dog error.

One handler asked me how to manage the lift when the fetch is not going to be directly toward the handler but rather back to the fetch line or to the center of the fetch panels. The lift should be in line with the fetch. In other words, if the sheep are set out exactly on the fetch line, then the lift should bring the sheep directly toward the handler. But if the sheep are being held off-line, then the lift should take the sheep toward the center of the fetch panels; this may require stopping the dog a little short or having him over-run slightly. The sheep's initial steps should be on the fetch line. This will avoid having to attempt a harder flank right after the lift, as you try to get them "back" on line. Remember, when it comes to having a controlled fetch, prevention is much better than cure.

Pace is the number-one factor in terms of the control you will have over the fetch line. If you do not establish a calm and steady pace from the outset, then all of your strategizing deteriorates into playing catch-up, and accurate work becomes next to impossible. Everyone wants to know what to do if the sheep run too fast. It is of fundamental importance from the outset that you do not allow this to happen.

When handlers ask me questions about the fetch, often they do not address the root cause of the problem. They ask how to slow the sheep, instead of asking why the sheep were

♠ FROM THE HANDLER'S POST ♠

running in the first place. Once the error at the top has occurred, it is extremely difficult to slow the sheep and regain control of both stock and dog. It is much more profitable to address that problem than it is to think about its consequences. The number-one cause of the sheep bolting off the top is the dog either chopping the top of the outrun or lifting with too much force, beginning a chase that gains momentum throughout the fetch.

An important strategy at trials, as I have said often, is to watch the runs that precede yours. Watch carefully how the sheep are responding at the top, whether they are heavy or flighty, whether dogs need to "stop short" or "over-run" in order to lift straight, how the sheep respond to too much pressure from other dogs. Careful observation before your run will help you to guide your dog so that the sheep WALK off the top, and "crisis management" and "damage control" do not become your main strategies.

During your own lift, make sure that you are watching the sheep. Most young handlers watch the dog too much and do not read carefully the signals that the sheep are sending. By watching carefully, you will see the sheep "gear up" for their movement, raise their heads, move their ears back. This is the most important moment in terms of your fetch. Unless the sheep are extremely heavy, I recommend the following: Just as the sheep lean forward to begin to move, *stop your dog*. Then immediately walk the dog in again. This will add just a tiny cushion of distance between the dog and the sheep, so that the dog is easing the sheep into motion instead of pushing them into motion.

This is an important concept some people do not realize. It takes less pressure to initiate movement for the sheep than it does to maintain movement for the sheep. In other words, the space between dog and sheep needs to be greater during the lift than during the fetch. Stopping your dog for a second not only gives you control over your dog, but also adds that tiny bit of distance that will allow the sheep to ease off the top instead of bolting.

Now, if the sheep do run, stopping your dog is seldom the best option for regaining control of the sheep. Stopping the dog is an emergency measure that might be required if everything has completely fallen apart and you need to regain control, but in terms of returning the sheep to the fetch line, you are basically "done" once you have stopped your dog. Because they often have a destination in mind, the sheep will probably keep going, and your dog will not be able to flank wide enough and far enough to get them back to the line.

Even when sheep are running, there is an ideal distance that you want to maintain be-

♠ FROM THE HANDLER'S POST ♠

tween sheep and dog so that you keep a governing hand over the sheep themselves. If you have a quiet, nice-working dog, then that dog can act as a magnet, holding the sheep back or slowing them as he brings them in. Now, this does not work for erratic or very pushy dogs, but a talented and quiet dog who is well-trained to maintain his own distance can "apply the brakes" from behind, if he is allowed to maintain contact with the sheep. If you stop the dog, you do not let this happen. So keep your dog up in the rigging, in control of the sheep, so that they do not race hell-bent for the exhaust pen, but rather are aware of and slightly worried about the dog that is behind them. In this way, you will make the most of your dog's abilities.

Another often-discussed technique for slowing the sheep down is flanking your dog. There are dogs that will flank smoothly enough and wide enough to get this done—but most dogs will not. If your dog will flank wide enough to slow the sheep without turning them, then you have a good dog and you have done a good job with your training, so this will be an effective technique. But most dogs will chop this flank slightly if the sheep are running, which will spook the sheep even further and cause them to turn rather than to slow down.

If your dog slices his flanks during the fetch, it is a guarantee that your fetch will happen too fast. And if your fetch happens too fast, it is likely that your dog is slicing his flanks. Again, newer handlers often blame the sheep, or wonder what to do about the running sheep, instead of wondering *why the sheep were running in the first place*. If your fetches tend to happen too fast, you should study your dog's flanking at home and make sure that he has not established bad habits of slicing or chopping those flanks.

Watch carefully, at home: as the dog flanks, he should maintain exactly the same distance from the sheep that he had while he was bringing the sheep. If you picture the sheep as the center of a circle, the dog should maintain the same radius from that center, following the circumference of the circle instead of making a straight line between, say, 12:00 and 9:00 on the clock face.

Another barometer you can use to see if your dog is chopping his flanks is the following: have him bring the sheep slowly and then flank him, watching the SHEEP very carefully instead of watching the dog. If the sheep jump, or spook, or bolt, or even change their pace a little bit, as they turn, then your dog has sliced that flank. It is important that you be hard on

♠ FROM THE HANDLER'S POST ♠

yourself at home if you expect to be successful at a trial.

The opposite problem occurs for some people: they flank the dog, who opens up wider and wider, trying to "beat the sheep to the barn," instead of holding in and turning the sheep efficiently. This is a difficult problem to correct. Either the dog has not been taught to hold in to pressure, or he naturally gives way to pressure. You can teach a "come-in" whistle that may help, and ideally you will realize that you have this type of dog very early in the training program. This type of dog should be made to stay with the sheep, to make tight turns, work in close spaces, and be comfortable closing the distance between himself and the sheep when he is told to do so. One other "emergency" strategy that may work during the fetch is the following: if for example the sheep are running to your left so that the dog is flanking "away to me" to bring them back to the line, and the dog is running too wide, give a quick "come bye" flank and send the dog in the other direction; when he gets behind the sheep, give a short "away to me" whistle again, and the dog has resumed contact with the sheep. But if you see this flaw in your dog, realize that you will have to work on this in all aspects of your training, from an early point, in order to overcome this habit.

♠ VERGIL HOLLAND ♠

Remember that if your run falls apart, it generally helps to study it, because it can reveal a problem you had not noticed at home. It can be beneficial to have an experienced handler watch your run, because your own assessment of why something happened may in fact not address the root cause of the problem. You are probably focusing on the specific trial situation instead of on the more general training problem which made you and your dog less able to handle the unexpected. Demand exactness, flexibility, teamwork, and perfection in your training, so that you can handle the sheep calmly and accurately at trials.

Of course, the fetch gates are there for a purpose and should not be disregarded. Stockdog trials are based on usefulness, on skills that are necessary every day in farm work. Putting the sheep through gates is an essential aspect of that work. In addition, stockdog competition is about accuracy and precision. To be among the top finishers at today's high level of competition, you must not only "hit" the fetch panels, but bring the sheep through the exact center of the fetch panels, and in a controlled style.

But if your dog brings the sheep straight and correctly off the top and the sheep are coming straight down the course, they are going to come between the fetch gates in any case. It

♠ FROM THE HANDLER'S POST ♠

can cause problems if you lose track of this priority—the lift, your dog's pattern of handling the sheep up to that point, and the first half of the fetch are the most important elements for hitting the fetch panels. Often handlers get too focused on panels, and this focus interferes with important last-minute commands. As one well known handler has said, handlers cannot stand "the pressure of non-intervention." Instead, your attitude should be to hold a straight and precise line for the entire fetch, successfully navigating the fetch panel obstacle along the way. The fetch panels, by regulation, are set twenty-one feet apart, but if the sheep are off-line by eight or ten yards throughout the fetch, you will lose significant points even though you do navigate the fetch panels safely.

One final point regarding fetch lines and pressures is that serious competitors must learn to watch the other runs at a trial. If you consistently see the sheep turn at one point or another during the fetch, you can be prepared to flank your dog accordingly, to act instead of react when you reach that same point in the fetch.

Remember that the sheep will respond differently to pressures after they have run the course once, so watching the first few runs will not necessarily prepare you for a run much later in the day. Often, if you are observant, you can see that the pressure is on one side of the field during the first part of the fetch (perhaps a shady area or an out-of-sight gate), and on the other side of the field once the sheep have come through the fetch gates (probably toward the exhaust pen). You will need to be ready for such shifts, so that you help your dog in time and minimize your loss of points. If you are going to navigate these hazards and maintain a true fetch line, the teamwork between you and your dog must be highly tuned.

This being said, there are certain hazards that can occur at the panels. I would like to point out some of the indicators of these potential problems and offer some advice as to how the handler can be prepared to manage them. The problems can be on the part of 1) the handler, or 2) the sheep, or 3) the dog.

Some handlers have "panel-phobia." A crucial aspect of successful trialing is that the handler must watch the sheep, constantly. Beginning handlers make the error of watching their dogs throughout the course, ensuring that the dog is following orders. Once you can trust your dog, you need to turn your attention to the sheep, both during training and during trialing. As the sheep near an obstacle (fetch gates, drive panels, pen), it is of particular importance to watch the sheep, to be tuned to their every indication of alarm or flight. Yet at this crucial

♠ FROM THE HANDLER'S POST ♠

moment, handlers tend to stop watching the sheep, and to watch the panels instead.

You must watch the sheep. Sheep almost always give some subtle indication of their next move. Your dog is tuned into these cues, and you must learn to be equally observant. Now, if the fetch has happened too fast and out-of-control, the sheep will not offer these cues, nor will you have time to observe them. So the first element is to have the sheep at a controlled pace, with your dog working calmly behind them.

If the sheep are proceeding nicely, then this is what to watch for: just as the sheep near the panel, if you observe them very closely, you will see that they may not exactly hesitate or stop, but they will indicate some alarm. Their ears come forward a little, which indicates that they are alerted to something. Alternatively, once they decide to pass through the panels, they stretch their noses forward just a little, and walk on through. You need to read the degree of their alertness. If they are very alerted, then they are seeing the fetch panels as a trap. Most of the time, just as you approach the panels, hit the brakes slightly on your dog. Don't necessarily stop him, but "tap the brakes"—set him back just a little, to release the "pushing" pressure on the sheep.

Alarmed sheep, at panels, react in the same way as sheep do at the pen. I make this comparison because handlers are more accustomed to reading this problem up close. As you know, if the sheep are at the pen gate, and the dog pushes too hard, the sheep suddenly act like the pen gate is more of a wall than an opening; they dart to one side or the other, refusing to enter the pen. How do you manage this? You stop the movement, hold your dog back, let the sheep look into the pen and realize that the gate is an opening; oftentimes, they then walk calmly into the pen.

You need to apply the same strategy at fetch panels (and drive panels). Just as the sheep approach the panels and show the first signs of alarm, ease back on the pressure and let them look through the panel opening. They will see "open field" on the other side, their alarm level will drop, and they will walk calmly between the panels.

Last-minute, panicky adjustments can raise the alarm level of the sheep. So if the pace is sedate and everything is going well, and you are not sure whether you should make an adjustment toward "dead-center," don't make it. If you are not sure what to do, do nothing! The minor deviation may cost you slightly, but a correction at this late moment can cost you much more.

Another important aspect of this is managing the fetch line immediately on the other side of the panels. As a judge, I see that many handlers

♠ FROM THE HANDLER'S POST ♠

lose more points in the twenty-five feet or so *after* the panels than they do in the rest of the fetch. This is because of the obstacle of the fetch panels themselves. They get in the way of your dog's flanking adjustments; the dog either over-flanks to get around a panel, or slices a flank to come between the panels. There are three elements necessary to avoid this problem: 1) have your dog in position (in relation to the pressure) just before the fetch gates, 2) come through the center of the fetch gates rather than near a panel, and 3) release the pressure ever so slightly as the sheep come through the fetch gates. Most of the time, calm sheep will continue in a straight line. Your dog can then follow them through the gates, in the correct position and in a settled manner and the fetch panels are no obstacle.

Sheep are individuals, just like you and your dog. The tendencies of the sheep are different at every trial, and each group of sheep reacts differently. But remember that sheep tend to indicate their next move. Handlers all work very hard at establishing perfect communication with their dogs, but many neglect the importance of reading the stock. My advice is that you practice with as many different kinds of sheep as you can. Travel, go to fun days and practice at other farms. This is mileage not only for your dog, but also for you. Don't just train your dog, train *yourself.* Learn to read the sheep's intentions, so that you are prepared to respond accordingly.

Western ewes can be extremely panel-shy. They see the panels as a trap. So with these type of sheep, you must set up the situation earlier. Set the dog back sooner than you would with other sheep; let the sheep look through the panels. If you see a head look one way or another, looking for a way out of the trap, then you had better have your dog back far enough, and ready to flank just a little, to block that potential exit. If a sheep indicates that she will try to turn, flank your dog quickly in that direction, and then flank him back to where he was, holding the pressure. It is important that you return him to his earlier position (assuming that that was correct in the first place); otherwise the sheep will take advantage of the opening he left, and go the *other* way. So flank your dog to cover the opening, turn that sheep's head back, and then get back in position in case the sheep try to go the other way.

We are talking about indications and movements that occur in a matter of seconds, so you must be quick and precise. But if you ignore the signs of alarm, and allow your dog to push too hard, the sheep will definitely scoot one way or the other around the panels.

♠ FROM THE HANDLER'S POST ♠

If your dog has been pushing the sheep too hard throughout the fetch—even if the sheep are not bolting madly, but just coming a little too fast—then the sheep are more likely to try to go around the fetch panels. Square flanking is of fundamental importance, throughout the fetch. You need to react just as soon as deviation from the fetch line begins to occur, rather than having to make a more drastic adjustment later. If your dog is back off the sheep and squaring his flanks, then you have complete control over the direction of the sheep's progress—you have "good steering power." Don't wait until just before the panels, to put the sheep on line. Keep them on line, all the time.

Also, your dog must be able to hold over to one side or the other. If you flank the dog, and he immediately tries to flop back to his original position (usually directly behind the sheep), then you are forced to repeat the flank and risk turning the sheep more than necessary. For straight lines, your dog must be trained to hold a flank properly—with exercises which must be done at home, for success on the trial field.

You should also practice by setting up fetch panels at home, remembering to move them around constantly so you do not create habits in your dog. Practicing with fetch panels at home helps in two ways: 1) it refines your ability to read the signs of alarm in the sheep, and 2) it helps you with the problem of depth perception, a significant factor. In training, it is important that you not necessarily run a whole trial course. Rather, if during the fetch something was "a little off," turn around and put the sheep back at the top, and repeat the fetch. If something is still wrong, repeat the fetch again. (Of course, this kind of repetition is for dogs that are quite far along in their training; this type of work is more about training *you* than about training your *dog*.) Figure out what the situation is that you are not reading correctly. Learning to read stock and terrain at home will serve you well in unexpected trial situations. In the end, remember that at a trial, the winners are the ones who can adjust to the particular field and the sheep, hold the lines, and hit the panels.

    Problems in the fetch can be caused by dogs who slice flanks (causing the sheep to veer in one direction or another), and dogs who open their flanks too wide (causing the sheep to go too far off-line before they are stopped and turned). Another problem that often shows up on the trial field is that the dog fails to cover the sheep appropriately; he just appears to follow along, but either doesn't flank far enough or doesn't "hold over" to the left or the right.

    This reflects that, even though the dog appears at home to follow your commands, moving in the "come bye" or "way to me" direction

♠ FROM THE HANDLER'S POST ♠

when you whistle, in fact the dog is working too much on his own. Everyone wants a "natural" dog, but you must remember that a dog will *naturally* do the wrong thing as often as he will *naturally* do the right thing! If you allow the wrong behaviors to become habits, then the dog will always be wrong. Bad habits seldom cure themselves "naturally." But if you teach correct habits from the start, then the dog will naturally do things right. Thus, even though this may seem like a contradiction, your attentiveness in the early stages of training will help you create a dog that is naturally correct—which keeps you out of a lot of scrapes in the more advanced stages of trialing.

If your dog tends to fall in behind the sheep and follow their drift, then you need to teach the dog to "hold the pressure," to hold a straight line behind the sheep *not* at the twelve o'clock position (if you are at six o'clock), but at the two o'clock or the ten o'clock position. This is not natural for most dogs. A banana-shaped fetch is much more "natural"! But if you are consistent in your training, and attentive to this critical skill, it is not difficult to teach your dog to stay in position, such that the sheep adhere to a straight line.

Some pressure-conscious dogs can feel very strongly that imaginary line between the sheep's current location and the place they would like to go. Those dogs do not want to stop until they reach that line; only then do they feel confident that they have blocked the sheep from a potential escape. When what you want is to tip the sheep back toward the fetch line, rather than to head them and stop them; you must have sufficient control to override the dog's instinct to go to the line of pressure. Your dog must understand what you are after, if he is not going to over-flank.

Handlers who are somewhat new to stockdog trialing might feel that their dog *had* to head the sheep, in order to stop them from running away. However, the sheep might not have attempted to defy the previous dog in this way, or the handler who follows you might appear not to have the same problem. This is probably not the result of "lucky draws," but rather the difference in the way that individual dogs establish and maintain their control over the sheep. The ideal dog, the most talented dog, is often able to control the sheep from behind. The sheep are worried enough about the dog that they do not try to escape. At the same time, the dog is holding back far enough that the sheep are not in a panic. This is the ideal situation for a fetch.

If the sheep break away and flee, so that your dog has to flank all the way around to stop them, then the problem may really have

♠ FROM THE HANDLER'S POST ♠

originated earlier, at the point when the sheep first decided to run away. This is important to consider when you review your own run, trying to figure out what happened and how to practice at home to avoid repeating this situation.

The most talented dogs seem to know naturally where they need to be, in terms of their distance from the sheep. They lift from the correct distance and then fall in behind the sheep or slightly off to the side as they begin the fetch. There is always a "right" distance, a point where your dog is close enough to hold them but far back enough to keep them relaxed. If, early in the fetch, your dog either pushes the sheep too much or holds back too far, then he creates a situation where the sheep defy him by trying to run away. This situation forces you to over-flank the dog, because the sheep will not stop for less. Once you over-flank, the problem becomes very difficult to fix. You cannot leave the dog where he is, because the sheep will either stop or turn too much, resulting in an off-line fetch. However, if you try to drop the dog back a little, you are in fact releasing the pressure, which then causes the sheep to bolt. Either way, you are set up for a losing situation. Once you allow the situation to build, one mistake compounds another, and you are really in a jam.

Often, during a fetch, the pressures in the field will shift. This is quite likely to occur in the region of the fetch panels. If your dog suddenly needs to shift to a new pressure point, but he has allowed himself to get positioned too far off the sheep, he will have to run much too far, much too fast, and still might not be able to maintain the sheep in a straight line. For minor and precise shifts in position, the dog has to be in close enough, so that short flanks have just the desired effect.

If this scenario sounds familiar to you, then the solution is not to be found on the trial field, but in the practice field. Your dog can be taught to put less pressure on the sheep, to increase his distance from them, never to take hold of them so tightly that the slightest release causes them to flee, nor to get so far away that he cannot catch them to turn them. At the end of this chapter, I will suggest some exercises that will help you and your dog reach this goal.

If you do find yourself in the situation where you have had to over-flank the dog in order to stop the flight of the sheep, and in the process he has gotten too far off the stock, then your best bet is to turn the sheep 90 degrees, right back to the fetch line. Hopefully this will bring your dog in, so that he regains his dominance and control. Then you can re-set your dog behind the sheep and resume an on-line fetch.

♠ FROM THE HANDLER'S POST ♠

Another type of dog that can find itself in this situation is a very quiet-working dog. If the sheep trust the dog too much, if they are *too* relaxed, then they might not bend as quickly when the dog flanks. They are not worried enough about that dog. In such a case, this dog has to flank much farther than would a different dog, in order to turn the sheep. There is no easy way out of this situation either. It just happens, either if your dog is quiet and non-intimidating, or if the sheep are just too "dogged" to feel threatened. Unfortunately, if you find this situation happening during the fetch, it will only compound itself during the drive, and you have a real problem on your hands.

Each trial in which you compete should serve not only as an event which rewards the best run of the day, but also as a learning experience where you evaluate your own training program and assess where you and your dog are, in relation to where you would like to be, as a team. So, if you have this problem during the fetch, you should watch the next run, and the run after that, and the class's winning run, and observe whether those handler-dog teams had the same problem. If they did, only then is it safe for you to blame the sheep or other conditions. But if they did not, then in some way you created the situation from which it was then difficult to extricate yourself. You might get it done, but it might not be pretty, and it will certainly result in a significant loss of points.

You might practice and practice in your field at home, watching lines and panels and learning to read sheep, but if you are always working in the same field, you and your dog will not be learning how to read the terrain, the lay of the land. This can make a tremendous difference in your ability to hold a fetch line on a different field, such as you might find at a trial.

Dogs that are accustomed to flat fields may be confused by hills; dogs who generally work on hilly fields may be put off by the deceptive distances of a flatter field. Being able to read the terrain during a trial, and to react accordingly, is a matter of mileage—both your mileage and your dog's mileage. As you first walk onto a trial field, you should be scanning the terrain to see how it will affect your work. Look up-field and question whether the sheep will go out of sight in a particular spot. In watching the first few runs—if you are fortunate enough not to be "first up"—you will have the advantage of watching how the sheep react to the terrain. For example, if the sheep begin the fetch by running down a steep hill, you can start to analyze how you will control their speed when your turn comes. If the sheep are spotted on the crest of a hill, you can watch the lifts and the stopping

♠ FROM THE HANDLER'S POST ♠

points of the other dogs, to see the best place to stop your own dog for a smooth, straight lift.

There are three particular terrain features that are fairly common at trials. One might be a fetch that occurs along the side of a hill, rather than straight down the hill. Another is an obstacle that the sheep must cross, like a stream or a gully. Finally, in many trials the sheep are temporarily out of sight, requiring particular handling strategies.

In the situation of a fetch along a hillside, the crucial factor is pressure lines—where the sheep are wanting to go. They may pull in either direction—high or low—depending on the location of the set-out and the exhaust, shady spots to which they are accustomed, or other factors. Watching the runs before your own can help alert you to this variable.

It is more difficult for the handler to gauge a straight line when the fetch occurs along a hillside, and sometimes more difficult for the dog to hold the line naturally. In terms of your own reading of the situation, focus on the direction of the sheep's heads rather than trying to tell whether the sheep are "high" or "low" on the slope. The sheep should be coming straight toward you—you should see their faces straight-on—throughout the fetch. As long as you stay focused on this, the terrain shouldn't be too much of a factor. (This is an element that is crucial to successful dog-trialing in general: your dog should be in your peripheral vision but should not be the primary object of your attention. To be competitive, to win trials, you need to focus your primary attention on the sheep rather than on the dog. You need to take for granted that the dog is slowing when you ask, stopping when you ask, and flanking when you ask; only then can you turn your attention toward the stock and the terrain—keeping an eye, occasionally, on your dog.)

If the sheep need to cross a stream or a gully, this can also make it difficult for you to hold a straight line. The sheep will often look for a particular point where they feel most comfortable crossing—the point of least resistance—and they will pull in that direction when they approach the obstacle. You can anticipate this, once again, by watching the runs before your own. Additionally, if this is a field where the sheep spend a good deal of time, you might see paths or worn areas that indicate a favorite crossing.

My best advice in this situation is that you walk out to that obstacle and examine it very carefully. Look to see how the footing is in the spot that is on the fetch line; see how the bank is constructed there; look for an existing path, especially one that would pull them off-line. You can anticipate this pressure-shift, and have your

♠ FROM THE HANDLER'S POST ♠

dog correctly placed in advance, so that the fetch line varies as little as possible.

In terms of strategy during your own run, you should focus on not hurrying the sheep across this obstacle. Slow your dog in advance, and let him work the sheep a little bit as they approach the creek or gully. Give the sheep a chance to look the obstacle over, and to make their decision about crossing. But just as soon as the first sheep begins to cross, stop your dog completely. If your dog follows them quickly into a ditch or stream, the sheep will panic and they will either blow in one direction or the other to avoid the obstacle, or they will bolt up the other side and be difficult to slow down again. This is similar to the situation at a pen gate; the sheep need to feel like this movement is their own decision, not a trap. If your dog is lying down at the appropriate distance, the sheep will pick their own way across and walk up the other side of the bank in a controlled fashion.

The third situation where terrain can pose difficulties is when the sheep disappear out of sight during the fetch. This gives many handlers nightmares well in advance of their run! But there are specific handling strategies that can help you navigate this problem area. The number one factor, as with the creek or gully discussed above, is that you walk out to that area and study the terrain. Look for factors that may draw the sheep one way or the other, while they are out of your sight. Next, you must know your dog very well. If your dog is driving and you cease giving commands, does your dog hold a straight line, tend to pull to the left, or drift off to the right? Try this in practice, and see how your dog reacts. This may also be how he will react during the fetch, when you suspend your commands. Many dogs, when the handler falls silent, "drop" the pressure and begin to follow the sheep in the direction that they want to go. You might be able to anticipate this by careful prior observation, and then, just as the sheep disappear from sight, give a counter-command to ensure that the dog will hold the flank or the line.

Your approach into an out-of-sight valley is the single most important factor in this type of fetch. If you know your dog's tendencies, set your approach accordingly, so that the dog is in the correct position. Then, plan on slowing the dog down, even if the sheep are already at a good, steady pace. Just as they dip out of sight, hit the brakes—or at least a slow-down whistle. Take the pressure off the sheep. This does not mean let the sheep go; rather, you are easing back on the pressure just a little, keeping your dog less worried, and letting the sheep relax and keep moving ahead. Then, the chances are that the sheep will re-appear exactly on line

♠ FROM THE HANDLER'S POST ♠

from where they were. On the other hand, if you get tense and nervous, your tendency will be to start giving "walk-in" whistles while the sheep are out of sight. You will have no idea whether the sheep have turned, whether the dog has flanked, or what has happened; your walk-in whistles may be worsening the problem, as the dog marches the sheep cross-ways down the gully!

So, the factors to remember are to know your dog, to set up your approach accurately, and to slow things down just as the sheep disappear—ease back just enough that the sheep do not feel the need to turn one way or the other. Hold the brakes, hold the line, and hold your breath!

In each of these chapters I try to recommend exercises which will help you, which give you the tools to handle the situations that might arise during a particular run. Of course, it is indispensable that you train on various kinds of sheep, in various fields, so that your dog learns that different groups of sheep react differently. You can teach your dog that the "right" distance is not a certain number of yards or meters, but rather something that must be felt, must be gauged, according to the heaviness or lightness of the sheep and the pressures built into the field.

In terms of reinforcing in your dog the idea of where to position himself in order to move the sheep in a straight line—how far he needs to flank without over-flanking—the best exercise I know is driving along a fence line. This teaches precision not only to your dog, but also to you the handler, as you learn to watch sheep's heads and ears, to stop your dog just at that point when he has flanked enough to hold the sheep onto the fence, but *not* so far that the sheep stop and look at him. The dog will soon learn the objective of this exercise, will learn to read the situation and the pressure, and will learn to position himself correctly. You will find that, driving in one direction, your dog can drop back to a position almost directly behind the sheep. But then, when you turn around and drive in the opposite direction along the same fence line, the dog might have to be in line with the sheep's ribs or even the front shoulder, in order to keep them from running. Therefore, this is a very good exercise to prevent over-flanking during competition.

Remember that your goal in this exercise is to keep the sheep walking. They should neither run nor stop. The dog will increase his attention and read stock closely, and so will you.

The other essential practice element is to practice many, many fetches. Of course, you cannot put too much pressure on the dog or let him get bored. Your exercises should be varied; you can stop to work on something else before

♠ FROM THE HANDLER'S POST ♠

coming back to the fetch. But the key here is not to do a huge number of fetches; rather, the emphasis you should have is that every single fetch should be perfect. So often I give lessons, and the handler is working very hard to do everything right, to be precise and to keep control of the situation. Then I say, "Okay, pick up the sheep and we'll go over there," and the handler relaxes, sends the dog with no set-up whatsoever, and lets the sheep come in sloppily. The handler turns things over to the dog completely, and the dog immediately senses that and loses all precision. This is a serious mistake. I try always to stop those handlers, and point out to them what they have just done. In your practice, every fetch needs to be a perfect fetch, if you want to have the control and accuracy that you need on the trial field. Make your dog toe the line, make the sheep come in on-line and at the right pace, every time.

If you are training a dog for competition, then you must be aware of the difference between "exercising" the dog and "training" the dog. You can only "train" if you are paying attention to each element, demanding correctness, and fixing problems when they occur. Your dog should learn something each and every time that you head out to practice. Your goal is *perfection*, in each lesson. Otherwise, he is just getting exercise, and while you might think that you are just having fun, you will most likely not have the same relaxed attitude when you don't do well in the next competition.

As a judge, I see many handlers lose a lot of points on the fetch, and I think this is due to the fact that they do not worry enough about this aspect of the dog's training at home. A border collie is bred to fetch sheep. This dog can be extremely useful on the farm due to his ability to bring the stock home. Handlers are generally quite confident that, if no problems are encountered on the outrun, if the sheep are held properly and the dog is in position behind them, then the sheep will somehow end up at their feet. And this is probably true—but the precision and correctness that today's competitions demand are not acquired by casual training, or by merely allowing the dog to develop his or her own instincts. Trial competition demands teamwork between handler and dog, such that the dog is willing at any moment to adapt his instinctual drives to the commands of the handler. In this regard, even though farm work really contributes to a dog's overall development, it *can* be detrimental to trial performance. If you are not careful, what is fine at home (banana-shaped fetches, chopped flanks, sheep moving a little too fast, dog and sheep responding automatically to the same pressures

♠ FROM THE HANDLER'S POST ♠

day after day) can be disastrous in trial competition.

The way to teach your dog to hold a flank during a fetch, rather than reverting to the habitual "twelve o'clock" position, is to set up your fetch practice in such a way that there will be pressure to one side or the other. For the sake of this example, we'll say that the sheep want to drift to the handler's left during the fetch, so you want your dog to flank "away to me" and stay over there, holding the sheep to a straight fetch line. Send the dog on the outrun, and once he has begun the fetch, give an "away to me" flank. Hopefully, the dog will flank. If he is a young dog, his tendency will then be to try to go back behind the sheep again. Just at the instant that he begins to head back in the "come bye" direction, lie him down. Then give another "away to me" command. You might find that you never give a "walk in" command during the entire fetch; just flanks and stops. The dog will learn to be comfortable holding that line, staying off the right or left flank of the sheep instead of directly behind. Once the dog realizes that this is what you are after, then fewer lie-downs will be required, and your dog will be more willing to hold the sheep in a perfectly straight line.

This can be reinforced during driving exercises; I recommend that you have the dog drive the sheep in a large oval pattern, with you at the center. Maintaining the oval will require that your dog hold the outside flank, continuously kicking out and staying off the flank of the sheep rather than always being behind them. Don't forget to keep balanced in this exercise; after driving an oval in one direction, turn around and drive an oval in the opposite direction, to keep the flanks evened up. But this exercise will help your dog be comfortable holding over on a flank, and will help your fetches as well.

Another exercise that is helpful for this skill is to have two groups of sheep in a fairly large pasture; you work the smaller group of sheep around the larger group. In the beginning, this would be a wearing exercise, but then could become a driving exercise as well. Using a separate group of sheep as a pressure source forces your dog to think more, rather than relying on his knowledge of habitual pressures such as a barn or a gate. If you wear one group of sheep in a large circle around another group, your dog must hold over to keep the two groups separated. As soon as his position is wrong—assuming he has some degree of natural ability—he will sense the problem, will know that he is about to lose the sheep if he is in the wrong place, and will automatically fix it. As with the driving exercise above, he will then learn not

♠ FROM THE HANDLER'S POST ♠

only to hold the flank, but to be *comfortable* in holding a flank.

A side benefit of these pressure-related exercises is that it allows the handler also to improve his "stock sense," his "feel" for how far the dog needs to flank, given certain terrain or certain types of sheep.

Remember that dogs, and border collies in particular, learn only by doing. The more different things they do, the more they learn. If they do the same thing over and over, they quickly form habits instead of reading the situation. Even dogs with a great deal of natural ability can become habituated, so that they get lazy about using that ability to the fullest. Border collies need variety in their work if they are to remain sharp. They need to be reminded that sheep headed downhill tend to speed up and that they need to keep track of the stocks' location even when the stock is temporarily out of sight. They need to be kept sharp by working the side of a hill, working steep or rocky terrain, spotting sheep that might look like stumps from a distance, and in general being ready for any "surprise" that a trial might offer. I can't stress strongly enough how important it is to work in different areas, even if you have to truck your own sheep to those areas; even the same old familiar sheep will act differently on new terrain, forcing your dog to stay alert and read the situation accurately.

Fun days are an excellent opportunity for refining and stretching your dog's ability to read terrain. Fun days tend to be fairly nearby, don't cost a lot of money, let your competitive edge relax a little, and allow you the opportunity to leave the post and help your dog if necessary. Sometimes they are held on fields that are a little too tricky for an official trial—too hilly, for example—and this is all good practice for your dog. Remember that every outing for a young dog should be viewed as a training exercise, not a competition.

Look for the most difficult terrain you can find—around barns, across rocks, through multiple gates, around rocks or other obstacles; learning to navigate these situations will build tremendous confidence in your dog and will also build your confidence in your own handling abilities. As a team, you and your dog will learn how to adjust your decisions to the terrain, and then you will not be thrown off-guard by new situations at trials.

6

The Turn at the Post

The first half of the turn is judged as part of the fetch; the second is judged with the drive.

Many handlers see the turn around the post as a necessary transition between the fetch and the drive but do not realize how important the style of the turn is, as regards setting the mood and the pace for the drive. The turn should not startle the sheep or excite the dog any more than necessary. Accurate reading of the sheep, a good knowledge of your own dog's habits, and a strong training foundation make this portion of the trial course a critical test of partnership and stock management.

Most judges agree that the first half of the turn is included in the scoring of the fetch; after the sheep pass behind the handler's post, any subsequent deductions are made from the drive portion of the score. Different judges have different rulings on whether all of the sheep must go around the post, or whether you may continue (certainly with a loss of points) if one sheep does not round the post correctly; handlers should ascertain this during the meeting, prior to the beginning of the class. However, in nearly all trials, a correct turn around the post—with at least some of the sheep—is required. Inaccuracy at the fetch panels or at the drive gates may result in a loss of points but often does not destroy the flow of your run. On the other hand, missing the turn at the post requires "unwinding" the sheep and making the turn correctly; this is usually very difficult, much more so than it is simply to do the turn correctly the first time. For this reason, handlers should be prepared—be very aware of their own advance plan for dealing appropriately with the situation (given the particularities of sheep and of field pressures) and should be in complete partnership with the dog, so that the turn is accomplished with as little disruption as possible.

A smooth line is your goal as you set up for the beginning of the drive. The most common pattern requires that the course line never crosses over itself; however, there are trials where either the pressures are so strong or the sheep are so people-shy that course directors

♠ FROM THE HANDLER'S POST ♠

have been forced to be more creative—either changing the direction of the turn or allowing a turn out in front of the handler's post.

The handler should prepare well in advance, in order to control the events that happen very quickly during the turn around the post. For one thing, the handler should be very aware of the direction for the turn. I will share here one trialing strategy that has been helpful to me. Most courses are run in one direction the first day, and in the other direction the second day; many, many handlers—myself included, of course—have done either the entire turn or a significant portion of it in the wrong direction! Clearly this is a costly error, and one from which it is difficult to recover. The tactic I recommend is that, before you send your dog (or just as the sheep come through the fetch panels, if you can remember at that time), make a habit of placing your crook in the hand that will be on the *outside* of the turn around the post—such that the crook will "push" the sheep around the post. Your dog will learn this signal, and you will as well, so that either the turn naturally flows in the correct direction, or you will realize the error in time to repair it. This trick works because it makes you conscious of the potential for error before it occurs. Another tip I recommend is that, either when you examine the course in advance, or as you reach the post, you study the angle from the post to the first drive panel. In this moment of tranquility, you can make observations that will keep you from later over-rotating in the heat of the moment.

A further step in "advance preparation" that is crucial, as with all phases of the competition, is the careful observation of the runs prior to yours. This is the best way to ascertain the type of sheep and the pressures at work on the course. You can learn from other handlers' mistakes and from their failures. While socializing is an important aspect of trialing, you will only become a competitive threat when you focus your intention primarily on study and preparation for your own runs.

The handler and dog must be a complete team during this portion of the course. In terms of your dog, there are three critical aspects: 1) Your dog must not slice his flanks when he makes this turn; if he fails to maintain his distance from the sheep, he will startle them and cause them to dart in the other direction or to be unsettled during the all-important set-up for the drive. 2) Your dog must not flank too wide at the post; this can cause as many difficulties as being too close, as it allows the sheep either to turn too wide, or else to escape, or even to think too optimistically about escaping. 3) Your dog must stop the flank exactly

♠ FROM THE HANDLER'S POST ♠

where you tell him to stop—neither early nor late—in order to set up appropriately for the line of the drive. Accurate and precise training at home, 100% of the time, will make it possible to avoid these three pitfalls during competition.

It is important to remember that you have taught your dog to maintain his distance from the sheep, at a constant radius. This can have an important effect on your turn. Stopping your dog well in advance of the post, thus increasing his distance from the sheep before you give the flank command, will create the probability of a very wide flank—sometimes too wide. Therefore, if a tight turn is required, you should walk the dog up closer to the sheep before giving the flank command. This will help the dog hold in where he needs to be in order to prevent a possible attempt at escape.

All too often it seems that the sheep are headed toward the post at a dead run! In such a case, all of the careful management strategies that you might have planned seem irrelevant. During this phase of the fetch, lying your dog down will *not* slow the sheep. Your only hope is to keep the dog in contact, at a precise distance from the sheep, hoping that he will be able to slow them down by the threat of his presence. Also, you can use your own body to block the sheep momentarily; flank the dog just as you step out of the way, so that the dog is always in position to control the direction of the sheep. In my opinion, drastic movements of the crook or arm-wavings are too risky. The sheep are only likely to become more alarmed. Rather, use the positioning of your dog as the primary tool to keep the sheep as close to the ideal line as possible.

In general, I advise that handlers not focus overmuch on the tightness of the turn; you should not necessarily always try to "leave wool on the post." An extremely tight turn will not get you any more points than will a slightly looser turn, and the looser turn will probably set you up better for your drive. If you try to make the turn too tight, the sheep may easily cross in front of you, requiring you to flank your dog back behind you in order to return to the line of the drive and risking upsetting the sheep in the process. Additionally, this will cost you a point or two, if the situation then requires that your dog pass in front of the post rather than behind it. As a judge, I have observed that over half of the handlers over-flank at the post and then must make the necessary correction.

Reading the sheep properly and responding accordingly are the real keys to managing the turn appropriately. Just as the handler uses his own body and physical presence at the pen and during the shed, the handler's positioning and movement can make all the difference in the

♠ FROM THE HANDLER'S POST ♠

tightness and smoothness of the turn. It is also critical to take into consideration both the type of sheep being used and the pressure to the exhaust pen, which is often quite strong as the sheep come around the post. Many runs are "made" or "wrecked" by how the handler and dog negotiate this dangerous spot.

Except in the case of very long fetches, I begin to set myself and the sheep up for the turn as soon as the sheep come through the fetch panels. For the best turn, it is necessary that the sheep give up on the idea of escaping toward the "wrong" side of the post well before they reach you. For example, in the case of a clockwise turn, the potential exists for the sheep to escape to the handler's left—this is the escape route that the dog must cover. But, if you can deter the sheep from this possibility *before* they reach the post, they will be less likely to "run for it" as they make the turn. This is of particular importance if, in the above example, the exhaust pen is located on your left. You and your dog can discourage this option throughout the second half of the fetch, and thus have more control. It is risky to push the sheep off-line as you accomplish this, but even if you have to do so a little bit, or widen your turn slightly, in order to anticipate and deter the sheep from bolting, this preventive measure may make the difference between losing the sheep and completing a successful run.

Then, when the sheep approach the post, you should be very aware of how your physical position can be used to assist in the turn. For example, if the sheep are very people-oriented, then you should stand very *close* to the post as they come past you. This will prevent the common practice of the sheep darting around in front of the post, or between the handler and the post. Furthermore, if the sheep are people-oriented and the pressure to the exhaust is strong, you yourself should step out in front of the sheep, very subtly and in a way that is not too obvious to observers, so that you are "leading" them around the post, drawing them to you. In this way, you are blocking the sheep and keeping their heads turned toward you, as the dog flanks. As they reach about the 4:00 position, or even later, you then step out of the way, toward the post, and allow your dog to complete the turn. This can result in a very smooth line, and also allows your dog that split-second of extra time to round the corner himself and keep the sheep from even thinking about an escape. Depending on pressures and where the dog begins the flank, this split-second can be all-important.

If the sheep are not people-oriented, then you can best help by moving a substantial distance

♠ FROM THE HANDLER'S POST ♠

away from the post, so that you are not pushing the sheep away, and thus widening the turn unnecessarily, by your own presence. You should still guard the post, but move around it evenly, so that the sheep maintain their own distance from the post and follow a smooth path as they turn. In addition, you should plan from the outset that your turn will be somewhat wider (as wide as necessary) in order to get the job done. At many trials, particularly in the West, the sheep are more afraid of the handler than they are of the dog; the result is that, as the sheep approach the post, they opt to defy the dog rather than risk approaching the handler. Many a run has fallen apart at this point. If you help here by moving away from the post and allowing the sheep to feel that they are getting past you, and also by tracing a wider path than usual, you can often overcome this hurdle.

If the sheep are both people-oriented and very sticky, a common problem is that they get "attached" to the handler. As the handler tries to get out of the way and the dog tries to begin the drive, the sheep are like Velcro, stuck to the handler's legs. In such a case, the best strategy is to include another stage in your turn: as the sheep come around behind the post, have the dog drive them away slightly—not directly along the angle of the first leg of the drive, but rather directly away from the post.

Only a short distance is required for this maneuver—maybe six to eight feet—then have your dog flank again, and put the sheep on line once they are a slight distance away from you. Then, if the sheep try to return to your feet, you have the space to flank your dog between yourself and the sheep and can begin your drive. In this case, you might visually think of the ideal path of the sheep as in the shape of a comma, laid on its side. Once the sheep reach the "tail" end, you turn them back and continue with the first leg of the drive.

The trialing tips offered above are intended to assist you with decision-making on the trial field. But of course, all the right decisions will not result in a successful run if you and your dog have not done your homework. At home, you can build into your dog the precision and accuracy that will allow you later to carry out your carefully-planned strategies.

This is one portion of the trial course that should be practiced very frequently at home, even at a very early point in the dog's training. As soon as the dog has mastered the basics of driving, you should have him bring the sheep to you, and then around you and into a drive. Of course, you should remember to practice this evenly in both directions and against all kinds of pressures. The dog will very quickly acquire the habit of looking to you for a direction and then

♠ FROM THE HANDLER'S POST ♠

of reading the sheep himself so as to assist as much as possible. He will also learn not to flank around too far and hold the sheep back to you—a common pitfall during Pro-Novice-level trialing. Practicing the turn is also very good for your own development as a handler, as it is an excellent opportunity to focus on reading stock and anticipating many of their sometimes-unwanted movements.

If you have a wide dog, be sure to have a "come-in" whistle or command that can be used when necessary. If you know that your dog has a tendency to slice flanks, use a "get out" warning as the sheep and dog come around the post. Practice with just a few sheep, and practice with a large group. The large group will help you and your dog develop your teamwork, since you will be largely responsible for covering the inside of the circle—not allowing any sheep to cross in front of you—while your dog covers the outside of the circle. The techniques will be entirely different with just a few sheep, and you can build maximum versatility into your dog by varying the practice exercises.

Finally, remember that practice does not make perfect; rather, *perfect* practice makes perfect. Do not make sloppy turns at home or allow your dog to be sloppy; imagine that every practice turn is being judged, and assign yourself the appropriate deductions. Furthermore, if the turn does not go well, you might want to move the sheep away a short distance and attempt the turn again, and again, until you figure out where your mistakes were (being careful, of course, not to stress or wear down a young dog). Your attentiveness will certainly be rewarded later, on the trial field.

7

The Drive

From the handler in a triangular direction with the dog in quiet firm steady control in straight lines through two gates and back to the shedding ring or pen area as required. An honest attempt must be made for each drive obstacle.
– 30 points

I would like to begin this discussion of the drive by comparing and contrasting this portion of the trial course with the fetch, in terms of necessary skills and potential problems. Many of the essential elements of a successful drive are the same as the elements of a successful fetch. As throughout the trial course, your priority as a handler should be on reading situations early, anticipating the actions of the sheep, and having your dog in the correct position to deal with those actions. Of course, the more talented your dog is, the more help you have in this regard; a talented dog will already be sensing the sheep's intended actions and will be more responsive to your commands, creating the smooth teamwork that is the foundation of a successful trial experience. Once you have established a line, a properly-trained dog with some natural ability should be able to hold that line to some degree, both during the fetch and during the drive. However, the better handler you become—in terms of reading the sheep and the situation— the more you will be able to help your dog to refine this technique.

The basic skills that we discussed in terms of the gather (outrun, lift and fetch) are also the basis for a successful drive: square flanks, the ability to hold against pressure rather than drop the pressure, and a steady pace. These are elements that must be taught during a carefully designed and consistent training plan. You must teach the dog these skills as he learns to gather, and then continue to teach them as you begin to train your dog to drive. A natural pace on the fetch, or the ability to hold the pressure, does not necessarily transfer automatically to the drive, as your dog progresses from the beginning level to a more intermediate stage of training; this is because the fetch goes along with the dog's natural instincts, while the drive—

♠ FROM THE HANDLER'S POST ♠

at first—is contrary to those natural instincts. On the other hand, as you teach your dog to be aware of pressures and to flank correctly while driving, you will notice a corresponding improvement in the dog's natural fetching ability. Thus the gather and the drive are two complementary skills, and they should be viewed that way as you design the training program for each individual dog. Your attention to these details throughout the training program, even through the Open level of trialing, will give your dog the necessary tools to handle whatever situations may arise during competition.

During the drive, the dog is pushing the sheep rather than following the sheep, and the sheep are less likely to be in a hurry than they are during the fetch. For these reasons, square flanks while driving are more difficult for your dog to learn than are square flanks during a gather. As regards pace, if your dog is pushy you will be more likely to lose control completely during the drive than you were during the gather. The gather pulls the sheep toward you, and you are more likely to be able to bring both dog and sheep under control. But the drive sends the sheep away from you and increases your dog's distance from you, so that the situation may progressively deteriorate. For this reason, it becomes even more important to have your dog under control, to be able to slow him down and relieve the pressure on the sheep, and to be able to flank without startling the sheep or creating a grip situation.

When we discussed the fetch, I stressed the importance of keeping your dog in contact with the sheep. Stopping your dog will not necessarily slow the pace of sheep in flight. This misconception has spelled the end of many runs for many inexperienced handlers. Your dog must be kept up "in the rigging," in contact with the sheep, in order to be in a position to catch them, even to head them if necessary, and to maintain or regain control. In contrast, if the sheep are particularly flighty during the drive, stopping your dog may be a very effective strategy. I call this the "bump and drift" method of driving. You walk the dog in enough to move the sheep forward, but stop your dog at the very instant the sheep begin to move off the dog. Then readjust your dog if necessary, flanking in order to control the direction of the sheep. Get your dog back on his feet again to push the sheep forward, but stop him before the sheep gain too much momentum. This tactic works very well with younger dogs, who may be over-zealous and push too hard. It also works well with more advanced dogs who may be particularly pushy. However, it does create a flow problem, and you can get in trouble with it. "Bump and drift" is not the ideal way to control a drive, but it is an

♠ FROM THE HANDLER'S POST ♠

important tactic to have to use when it seems necessary at a particular stage of the dog's training or on particular sheep. It can keep things from getting out of control as you learn to perfect the drive.

We have discussed the importance of reading the sheep and reading the terrain during the gather so that you can anticipate the pressures and the problems. This becomes even more important during the drive. The dog is relying much more on the handler during the drive than during the fetch; he does not have the assistance of as much natural ability in terms of reading pressures. For this reason, it is crucial that you study the field ahead of time, watch other runs if possible, and be ready to respond to the particular conditions of the trial field. It is also crucial that you concentrate throughout your run and maintain control every minute. You should never rely on luck, hoping that the sheep will return to the line on their own, hoping that a wobble will correct itself and not get out of control, hoping that the dog or the sheep will slow down rather than accelerate. During trial competition, you make your own luck. If the sheep are moving off line a little, it is because your dog is not in the correct position, and you should repair that situation immediately. You must force yourself to react at the moment you begin to see any deviation from a straight line.

Remember that you are the one at the wheel; your attention and your response time make the difference between a successful and an unsuccessful run.

During the fetch, it is fairly easy for the handler to see the correct line. As previously mentioned, before you ever send your dog, you should pick an object directly behind where the sheep are spotted to serve as one end of your sight-line. The fetch line is directly from that object to the *center* of the fetch panels, and from the center of the fetch panels to you. This same tactic works during the first leg of the drive. You should remember to check that line, once the sheep are moving off you at the post. Look ahead, from the post to the *center* of the first drive panels, and make a mental note of the line. Then re-check that line throughout the first part of the drive, looking ahead repeatedly and making sure that you are headed directly toward the center of those panels. It is a common mistake for handlers to feel that making the panels *at all* is a victory and to aim only for the general vicinity of the panels; this causes a lot of near-misses and a lot of lost points. The successful handler must aim for perfection, and then achieve as close to that goal as possible.

During the crossdrive, the line is more difficult to sight. You should establish that line for

♠ FROM THE HANDLER'S POST ♠

yourself before the class begins, preferably by standing at the post and having someone else walk it for you. Then, by watching other runs (if possible), you can improve your chances of staying on the line. As you know, fields can be very deceptive, but by watching enough runs, you can give yourself a real advantage. Throughout the crossdrive, you should do two things: 1) repeatedly look behind the sheep to the first panels as well as looking ahead to the crossdrive panels, in order to re-establish for yourself the line of the drive. If you have strayed above or below it, it is very important that you return directly to it, rather than having a banana-shaped crossdrive line. 2) Remember that the sheep should almost always be perpendicular to you; if you see noses or hind ends, the sheep are probably not on the crossdrive line. This, of course, applies only to "typical" drive courses where the two sets of panels are equidistant from the handler's post. If the sheep are quartering away from you, or quartering toward you, this must be corrected immediately; it generally will not fix itself.

As we all know, seeing the line is one thing and staying on it is quite another. One key strategy to remember, as you practice at home and during trials, is that two flanks of the same length will not create the same reaction in the sheep. Instead, the sheep's reactions to a dog's flank depends on the pressure situation *at that moment*. For example, let's say that you are on the first leg of a left-hand drive, and there is strong pressure to your left (e.g. a barn or the exhaust pen). Your sheep are too far toward the middle of the field, and you need to give your dog an away-to-me flank in order to rectify this. You are thus turning the sheep *toward* the pressure. You should realize this consciously and know that a shorter-than-usual flank will be required. In addition, you should know that the sheep may well over-correct and you should be prepared with an immediate come-bye flank afterwards, in case they do turn too far to the left, toward the pressure. The reverse is also true; let's say that in the above situation (left-hand drive, pressure to the left) your sheep have strayed too far to the left, toward the pressure. Your dog will need to flank *more* than usual, in order to divert the sheep from this pressure source. Then, if you do over-flank with this come-bye whistle, you should be prepared with a *very* short away-to-me corrective. The corrective flank must be a very minimal one, or you will be inviting the sheep right back to that pressure. In that situation, a longer flank to the come-bye side, and then a very short away-to-me whistle (a flank only half the distance of the previous one), should re-establish the line of the drive. In this example, you need only half the

♠ FROM THE HANDLER'S POST ♠

flank when flanking toward the pressure as you need when flanking away from the pressure.

Finally, in terms of accuracy during the drive portion of the course, I will reiterate what so many judges say at handlers' meetings: the third leg of the drive is as important as the other two legs! Many, many handlers drop their attention after making the turn at the crossdrive panels. This is partly because the handler is turning his attention to the pen, getting to the pen and opening the gate, watching the set-up for the pen, etc. The other reason is that the dog is basically in "fetch" mode during this leg of the drive; he is bringing sheep home and needs fewer commands to do so. And it is true that without your help, the dog will most likely get the sheep to you. But he will not hold the same kind of accurate line that you were requiring during the other parts of the drive. One important thing to remember is where the line is on this third leg of the drive. Many handlers unconsciously have the sheep travel a straight line from where they turn after the crossdrive panels to the pen. However, the sheep might have travelled a good distance past the crossdrive panels before turning. Or, they may have made a particularly wide turn at those panels. Even worse, they might have missed those panels. In any of these cases, it is important for you to glance back to the crossdrive panels as the sheep travel back home. Remember that the correct line is from the panels to the pen—not from some imaginary point beyond the panels. Watch a few runs and trace that line in your own mind from the panels to the pen, and you will begin to notice how many people allow the sheep to stray from that line and thus lose valuable points during this portion of the course. Keep the same control over your dog that you had during the first two legs of the drive; keep the same level of attention to accuracy and lines; don't worry so much about the pen until the sheep get to that area of the field.

Mastering the drive is probably the most difficult part of training and trialing, for both the dog and the newer handler. It requires a firm training foundation, a great deal of trust on the part of dog and handler, an ability to read stock and anticipate situations, and the ability to concentrate one hundred percent on what is happening. The only way to lessen the possibility of losing control of your sheep (or dog) during the drive is to correct the small problems before they become big problems. Adjust for minor deviations from the line, so that you do not need to make a major correction; slow your dog before the sheep run rather than after; and anticipate what will happen rather than reacting to what has happened.

♠ FROM THE HANDLER'S POST ♠

The pace is the single most important element of the drive. The ideal pace is a fast walk or a slow trot, and trial courses should set the allotted time according to this ideal. You must therefore read the sheep in order to keep the dog exactly at the right distance to move the sheep at that pace, without spooking them into speeding up. Establishing this pace is the only way that you can give yourself time to look ahead and back, check your lines and encourage your dog to flank squarely and accurately so that he is not attempting to catch fleeing sheep.

The judge is also looking for this ideal pace. If your sheep are moving too fast, the points deductions will generally take care of themselves; you will miss a panel, or lose control altogether. If the sheep are moving too slowly, or grazing during the drive, the judge may deduct points for this. In addition, it is likely that you will run out of time before completing the course. The optimum trial performance is to move the sheep in a workmanlike and efficient manner, completing the tasks with minimal stress to the stock, and with maximal accuracy.

While properly-paced sheep will most likely flock fairly well during the gather, it is more likely that one will attempt to stray from the others during the drive. This is because the dog is not exercising quite as much control during the drive as during the gather and doesn't have quite the level of natural ability to anticipate that one sheep may have a different "flight plan" than the others. It is also because during the gather, the sheep may sense or know the location of the exhaust pen and thus intend to travel in your general direction anyway; but during the drive, they may decide to head back to the set-out pen, inviting disaster for your run. In these cases, the dog is relying more on you to help manage the situation than he was during the gather. The dog must have total trust in what you are saying in order to establish and maintain the line. If you see one sheep looking up toward the set-out pen or across to the exhaust pen, you should take immediate steps to help your dog prevent a split, rather than relying on your dog to the degree that you might during the fetch. As you continue to improve your own ability to read the sheep, your dog will learn that all of your commands have a purpose, and that you are helping the dog to stay out of trouble. This is the way that true teamwork will develop so that you do not have to force your dog to flank; the dog will learn to comply rather than fight you, his pace will naturally become more controllable, his flanks will naturally become more accurate, and your drives will fall into place.

♠ FROM THE HANDLER'S POST ♠

If the only time you practice driving in straight lines is at a trial, the degree of teamwork required for winning will never develop. Many handlers practice controlling the pace at home, but do not practice straight lines or hold themselves to the correct standard of accuracy. You do not need to set up panels in order to practice driving in straight lines; landmarks such as trees or rocks are just as effective. However, it is easier to "fudge" when using natural landmarks; some of my students have been known to change their destination once the sheep are too far off line, and just head for a different fence post or clump of trees. For this reason, while practicing panels at home may or may not help your dog, setting up panels may well help *you*. Once panels are set up, you are forced to become the judge of your own drive and to try to maintain a level of accuracy that should ideally be a part of all of your training. Driving to panels will improve both your whistle-eye coordination and your depth perception; it will also help you learn to use very short flanks, to make minor adjustments in order to preclude the need for more major adjustments later.

There is a danger that you will make your dog too comfortable with a particular set-up in using panels at home. You will feel as if you and your dog are improving daily, when in fact he is just learning how to drive that particular course, in that particular field, with those particular sheep. This can give you a false sense of security and can diminish the flexibility in your own training. It is crucial that you move the panels around; this is important both for your own development as a handler and for your dog's development. Put the panels in different places where the pressures will vary. Or reverse your usual patterns: instead of coming home after the crossdrive, turn right around and crossdrive in the other direction. Sometimes you may want to set up just one panel, to practice a tight turn around it. These constant variations will keep the dog from taking matters into his own hands and assuming he knows what you are after as soon as he sees panels. Some handlers brag that their dogs have learned to head directly for the panels while driving. This can be good occasionally, but it will more often cause harm; for example, I have seen dogs that spot the fetch panels during the crossdrive, and head the sheep directly for them, regardless of the handler's desperate whistles to the contrary! Other dogs, who have been trained only to drive in the pattern of a triangle, will anticipate that last flank at the crossdrive panel and turn early, thus causing near-misses. You do not want your dog to learn to work independently of you on the trial field, and in order to prevent this, you

♠ FROM THE HANDLER'S POST ♠

need to vary the practice situations so that patterns do not develop.

Practicing at home will also train you about the subtleties of whistling commands across a greater distance. The reaction time increases as the distance increases, so that it takes longer for the dog to hear, interpret, and respond to a flank whistle. This means that you must anticipate to a greater degree, both in issuing the flank command and in following it with the stop whistle or voice command; you should whistle or shout "lie down" a second *before* you actually wish the dog to stop, just *before* the sheep's heads turn in the desired direction. This will prevent over-flanking and will prevent you from having to play "catch-up."

8

The Pen

On completion of the shed the handler shall proceed to the pen, leaving the dog to re-unite the sheep and bring them to the pen. The handler will keep hold of the gate rope (six feet long) until the dog works the sheep into the pen.
– 10 points

The pen is one phase of work which is included at every level of trial competition—from Novice-Novice through Open. The reason for this is that penning is one of the most-used skills on the farm or ranch. In "real life" we are always putting stock into barns, through gates, into trailers, etc. In all of these tasks, the object is not to bring stock to the handler, but rather to push the stock *past* the handler. It is important for beginning handlers to realize how difficult this is for the young dog, how alien it is to the dog's natural gathering instinct. However, once the dog understands this type of job in the real world—for example, at gates or barn doors—then he grows much more comfortable with it. Easing sheep into a free-standing pen, in stockdog competition, should be seen as merely an extension and a refinement of that fundamental skill.

Penning and shedding are also two of the most technically demanding aspects of the competition, in terms of the precision required, the accuracy of timing and distance, and the importance of the handler's ability to read sheep. Close work such as penning and shedding also requires a different kind of relationship between dog and handler. While through the rest of the course the handler is the "driver," giving directions and guiding the dog in terms of speed and direction, at the pen the dog and handler have more equal tasks. The handler must do his or her part to guard the "gate side" of the pen and not allow the sheep to sneak between handler and gate. During this phase of work, then, the handler is working the sheep directly, instead of just working the dog. This requires the handler to approach this task with a different mindset—to be prepared to move appropriately, to apply or release pressure

♠ FROM THE HANDLER'S POST ♠

himself as needed, while never losing concentration on the dog and sheep.

Close work is in one way easier, and in another way more difficult, than the "distance" aspects of the course. On the one hand, the dog is physically near the handler during the pen and the shed, and thus the handler may have slightly more control than in the longer-distance phases of the course. On the other hand, the dog is also closer to the sheep, applying more direct pressure; this situation creates tension in the dog (which can cause him to slice a flank or even to grip) and also in the sheep (increasing the likelihood that they could blow apart and get past you or your dog).

Another aspect that adds difficulty to the task of penning is often the proximity to the exhaust pen and the resulting increase in pressure. Sheep are likely to know where the exhaust pen is and will do their utmost to get there, especially after the first day of the trial. Therefore, your dog's ability to read and react to pressure, and your ability to understand the concepts of pressure and balance, will always be tested at the pen.

The ability to pen is critical to success in stockdog trialing. In terms of competition, ten points is a large piece of the overall score; serious competitors need to plan not only to get the sheep penned, but to achieve a perfect score—or as many points as possible. The objective is not just to end up with all of the sheep in the pen, but to accomplish the entire task in a professional and workmanlike manner, with as little stress as possible on the stock, and with maximum efficiency in terms of time. In USBCHA trials, the pen is often the last or the second-to-last phase of work, which adds the pressure of the time clock. Those who determine the appropriate number of minutes for completing the trial course do so with the intention of requiring efficiency. If the time limit is set correctly, and if you have not rushed the sheep through the course, you will not have a lot of time at the pen. Even if the pen is the second-to-last task rather than the final one, the competitive handler must be sure to leave the maximum amount of time to accomplish the shed afterwards; therefore, there is still pressure to pen the sheep quickly, and to lose as few points as possible in the process.

For a successful pen, the sheep must be trapped between you and your dog, so that their only avenue of escape is to walk into the pen. However, the sheep must not feel too trapped, or they will panic and refuse to go into the pen. This is the delicate balance that the dog and handler must strike in order to execute a ten-point pen.

♠ FROM THE HANDLER'S POST ♠

In addition to earning maximum points in minimal time, there are other advantages to penning successfully on the first attempt. For one thing, once the sheep have been able to go around the pen once, they are more likely to attempt it again—they have learned the escape route. Additionally, the first attempt at the pen has the advantage of a long set-up process; the handler begins to set up for the pen after the sheep make the final turn from the drive or the wear, thus guiding the sheep along a straight line that leads directly toward either the gate or the back corner of the pen. Second and third attempts do not offer that luxury of a long set-up. Instead, the sheep are often hugging the pen or breaking for the exhaust, requiring more complex and risky strategies on the part of the handler.

The size of pens for USBCHA-sanctioned trials is standard; regulation size is 9 feet x 8 feet. This is a change from the proportions of years ago, which were 3 meters x 2 meters (9'9" x 6'6"), and while the square footage is not significantly different, the new size allows for a wider (8 foot) gate opening. Pens should be escape-proof, approximately four feet in height, preferably made of wooden planks or pipe gates, and with the planks or pipes close enough together so as to prevent smaller sheep or lambs from slipping through. Solid-sided pens are somewhat forbidding for sheep, and all-wire pens are also more difficult, because the sheep do not perceive the walls of the nearly-invisible pen as a "safe space."

Course directors should try to make sure that the gate swings freely, on hinges if possible. Ideally the gate should be able to open more than 90 degrees. Although I don't generally advocate that handlers actually open it any farther than that, there are situations where being able to swing the gate farther can prevent an escape. To the gate should be attached a six-foot rope which is easy to pick up, and the construction of the pen should be such that the gate can swing from either direction, in case a change of position or direction is required.

Correct placement of the pen is extremely important in the designing of a trial course. I have seen many trials in which successful penning is made nearly impossible, particularly for less experienced dogs and handlers, because of the way the pen happens to be turned. I have heard some judges and course directors claim that the pen must face in a certain direction for best spectator visibility, or perhaps so that the judge can see the mouth of the pen. However, the pen *must* be placed in the spot and direction most appropriate for the success of the competition—even if this means that the judge must step out of the trailer in order to see completely. And correct pen orientation can

♠ FROM THE HANDLER'S POST ♠

only be achieved by someone who knows and understands the pressures of the field, the exhaust pen, etc.

The governing rule is simple: the pen *must* be positioned so that the dog is guarding the "pressure side" of the gate. In other words, the handler's side—the side with the hinges—must never be the direction to which the sheep most want to escape. Since in general the strong pressure is to the exhaust area, this means that at most trials, the dog should be guarding the path between the pen and the exhaust. If the handler is all that stands between the sheep and the exhaust, the sheep will win, almost every time.

This makes very obvious sense, once it is stated clearly. I hope that all course directors will take a moment to examine their trial courses, to ensure that they have not jeopardized the handler's entire run—especially in classes for less experienced handlers. Disqualifications, injuries to stock, over-worked dogs, and disappointed handlers are inevitable if the sheep are difficult and the pen is improperly set. And the situation only worsens as the day wears on and the sheep grow wiser to the odds in their favor.

Following this guideline, and assuming that the gate can be hung so as to swing from either side, the course director has two choices.

The first is that the sheep can be brought from the drive/wear directly into the mouth of the pen. In such a case, the line of the course is from the lower edge of the crossdrive panel directly to the center of the mouth of the pen. The second choice, which often makes the pen easier to achieve, is to have the back of the pen facing the crossdrive panel, so that the sheep are brought to the back corner of the pen and along the outside; the dog then makes one last wide flank and tips the sheep into the pen, and the handler walks across and closes the gate. In this case, the line of the course is from the lower edge of the crossdrive panel directly to the inside back corner of the pen. This positioning allows the sheep fewer opportunities to escape, as they are guided along a kind of invisible "chute" that runs between the pen and the dog.

Handlers who feel proud of having penned their sheep are often surprised to find out how few points they earned in doing so! The judge has a "perfect pen" in mind, and only the perfect pen can earn a full ten points. Any deviation from the following scenario (unless the judge is lenient to allow for difficult sheep) will result in a less-than-perfect score at the pen.

Your set-up for the pen should begin as you make the turn through the crossdrive panels. You must have accurate direction and accurate

♠ FROM THE HANDLER'S POST ♠

pace during the third leg of the drive, both for full drive points and for the correct set-up for your pen. In terms of line, any deviation from "straight" will be likely to interfere with your pen set-up. The ideal pen involves bringing the sheep in at the correct angle. In terms of pace, if the dog rushes or slices that last turn, or if the sheep bolt away during that last leg of the drive, it is likely that the sheep will not be settled enough for a smooth pen.

The judge will have a spot somewhere along that line where he stops judging the drive and begins judging the pen. However, the two phases of work are inseparable; an error in one almost always leads to an error in the other. Therefore, you should think about and prepare for the pen at the moment you make that last turn in the drive.

In the Novice-Novice class, the pen often takes place after a short "wear." In this case, the crucial element for the correct approach to the pen is that, if at all possible, the handler stops the sheep at a certain distance from the pen—stop your dog, and then use subtle crook motions to discourage knee-knocker sheep from following you. Then go to the gate, get yourself into position, and continue with the pen.

Many handlers lose their concentration as they move from the post to the pen. They may have to turn around and find the gate rope, or figure out how the gate opens, as well as to prepare mentally for the next task—it is easy to understand why handlers tend to lose so many points and allow careless errors. However, successful competitors must not allow this to happen; they must maintain the same precision during the final phase of the drive/wear as they did during the earlier portions.

The pen involves the sheep approaching the pen at the correct angle and at a steady and settled pace. All sheep should be looking in the same direction. If the sheep stop in the mouth of the pen but do not turn around, there will probably not be a deduction of points; but if the sheep turn around to face the dog or the handler, points will be deducted. Two possible errors can cause the sheep to turn around: too much pressure, or too little pressure. Both dog and handler must exert just the right pressure so that the sheep "decide" to walk into the pen. Two fundamentals of stockdog work control this last phase of penning: *read the sheep* and *read the pressures*. When the handler closes the gate, making sure that it makes contact with the side of the pen, the task is complete.

For Novice-Novice handlers, the first try at the pen is of critical importance. Once the sheep have begun to ring the pen, the average young dog and inexperienced handler have little chance of success. Therefore, my advice to

♠ FROM THE HANDLER'S POST ♠

novice handlers is to take all of the time and caution necessary to set up a pen that will be successful on the first attempt. As discussed above, this means having the sheep well settled before they begin their final approach to the pen. It also means having a dog that understands the task of penning, that will flank off-balance without slicing, and that will not try at the last moment to run to the back of the pen, thinking that the sheep are "escaping!"

The pen and the shed are two tasks during which it is critical that the dog have a real understanding of the job he is facing. At the pen, a "push-button" dog (one who follows commands but is not thinking on his own or using his instincts) will almost always over-flank. This causes the sheep to turn not into the mouth of the pen, but a little further, so that they sneak past the pen opening and escape along the outside of the pen. The well-trained dog, on the other hand, will be prepared for the stop whistle, will himself feel the exact spot at which he should stop, and will turn the sheep's heads directly toward the gate hinge; from there the sheep will easily walk into the pen.

Reading the sheep is critical once you and the dog have positioned them in the mouth of the pen. Study the heads of the sheep; sheep tend to follow their noses. If two sheep are looking into the pen but one is looking just outside, eyeing a possible escape, I advise you not to trust your luck. Do not just hope that that sheep will change its plan and follow the other two. Instead, give your dog that very short flank command—ensuring that he neither slices in nor over-flanks—and tuck that sheep's head back around, before doing anything else. If you have set up the correct training program, your dog will already be watching that sheep and will be prepared to make that short flank to cover them.

Sometimes, that single sheep will escape in spite of your best efforts. In such a case, your strategy should be to close the gate partially so that the penned sheep are discouraged from escaping (remembering that once you close the gate fully, your run is over). Block the remaining opening with your body. Then, even if it involves making a full circle around the pen, if you are a Novice handler, I advise that you have your dog take the single past you, around the back of the pen, up the side and toward the narrow gate opening. As the single approaches, open the gate just wide enough to invite the sheep in to join the others. Throughout, your dog must be flanking widely enough not to panic either the penned sheep or the single sheep. Of course, Open handlers should do whatever is necessary to avoid having the single sheep circle the pen

♠ FROM THE HANDLER'S POST ♠

completely, in order to minimize the loss of points.

We stated earlier the ideal pen gate should be able to be opened more than 90 degrees. This will allow the handler a critical step backwards, should one be necessary to block an escape. However, I generally do not recommend that handlers open the gate more than 90 degrees, for three reasons. First, a 90-degree opening allows the handler to construct the longest possible visual barrier, comprised of the gate, the rope, the handler's outstretched arms, and the crook. Once the gate is opened further than 90 degrees, the handler cannot block the pressure as effectively. Second, the wider the gate is opened, the wider the arc that the dog is forced to cover. If the gate is opened too wide, often the sheep escape in the other direction, because the dog is too far out of position to stop them. And finally, if the handler does bring the sheep to a stop in front of him, but the gate is open too far (beyond 90 degrees), it is not as easy to "tip" the sheep directly into the pen; there are too many possible directions open to them.

Another penning tip that is useful to some handlers is to open the gate only partially, while the sheep are further away, and then draw it open more fully as the sheep get close. I find this particularly helpful if the sheep are accustomed to being penned. If they see the pen gate opening, they know what comes next, and they are thus drawn into the pen more quickly and with less chance of hesitation. On less-broke sheep, I have not found this trick to be as beneficial; rather, I advocate opening the gate 90 degrees and concentrating fully on the sheep's approach.

If the pen is placed such that its back is toward the third leg of the drive, you can use this to your advantage in various ways. One method that I have found particularly helpful is to use the pen as an obstacle, to slow down sheep that are coming too fast. As they come along that third leg of the drive, aim them directly for the back of the pen. They will see this as an obstacle in their path and will naturally slow down. Of course, like many "tricks," this requires great precision and some risk; the sheep, once they see the obstacle, are as likely to swerve to one side as to the other. You must have your dog in position so that the sheep do not dart around the wrong side of the pen, thus costing you points on your approach.

Of course, we all hope to pen the sheep on the first attempt. But in case that does not occur, the competitive handler must have strategies for setting up the second attempt. Of fundamental importance is the psychological aspect: you must not give up or lose your

♠ FROM THE HANDLER'S POST ♠

focus. Do not blame your dog or get in a hurry. Instead, think strategically. First and foremost, plan how to conserve your dog's energy. I have seen so many handlers send their dog around and around, trying to catch the sheep's heads. As the handler gets more frustrated, the dog gets wider and wider. Once your dog is too tired, he will not be able to pen. So, send him to catch the fleeing sheep, but as soon as the sheep are turned back in the direction of the pen, stop your dog and assess the situation. This will allow the sheep to settle, allow your dog to rest, and allow you to formulate your strategy.

Do not stop your dog, however, if the sheep are moving *away* from the pen. This will only make a bad situation worse. Many novice handlers use "lie down" as a coping mechanism; as soon as the sheep bolt, the handlers feel compelled to stop their dogs. This invites defeat. Catch the sheep, turn them back, and *then* stop your dog.

You now have the chance for a second approach to the pen. For this approach, set-up is as important as it was for the first attempt. Gauge the pressures and figure out which way to bring the sheep in order to maximize your chances for success. Competitive Open handlers try to bring the sheep in a direction that will cost them the fewest points, but they have quick, well-trained instincts and quick, well-trained dogs. Novice handlers should not think about points at a time like this; they should think about success. This means, in general, not trying to bring the sheep back around the handler side of the gate—the arc that the dog must cover is too wide. Rather, bring the sheep up along the non-gate side of the pen, and then tip them in.

There is a precise distance from the sheep that the dog needs to maintain. If the dog is too close and the sheep are panicked, it is unlikely that the pen will be accomplished. On the other hand, some inexperienced handlers have a tendency to push their dogs out too far at the pen. This creates two problems: 1) the dog has to run too far to catch the sheep quickly, and 2) the dog does not exert enough pressure to put the sheep through the gate. An awareness of this should be a part of your at-home training program.

As far as training for the pen, we have stated throughout this chapter that it is critical that the dog have an understanding of this task. The dog must know that he is to bring the sheep not *to* you, but *past* you. This is a skill that can be taught not only by training with a free-standing pen, but also by working sheep through gates, by loading trailers, putting sheep into the barn, etc.

♠ FROM THE HANDLER'S POST ♠

When you move sheep at home, don't just open a gate and have your dog push the sheep through. Rather, close the gate; then open it a little; let a few sheep through; back the dog off and close the gate; have the dog re-apply the pressure as you open the gate again, and let a few more sheep through. The dog will thus learn what you are setting him up for, when you stand at a gate, whether at home or at a trial. He will learn how to react when one sheep breaks away—how to tuck it back in and hold the pressure steady. He will learn how to "go back" or release pressure without perceiving that as a reprimand. He will learn not to slice flanks, and he will learn how to push sheep with just enough force to start them walking; then, finally, he will learn to stay put once the sheep are going through the gate.

As stated above, reading the heads of the sheep is critical; however, if your dog is not trustworthy, you cannot have your full attention on the heads of the sheep. Your dog's reliability is built up not on the trial field, but on the practice field. Test yourself and your dog in the following way: wear a hat with a brim low over your eyes and try to pen the sheep in such a way that the hat brim completely blocks your view of your dog. See if you can gauge the appropriate commands based solely on the actions and reactions of the sheep, rather than on studying your dog's position. Ensure that your dog is not coming in closer and closer with each flank command. This kind of training yardstick can help you to plan future practice sessions, by highlighting areas for improvement.

If your sheep are too pen-broke, your dog can lose his "edge" and be caught off-guard at the next trial. If you really want to test your dog at home, and your sheep are too tame, try tying another dog to the back wall of the pen. (Of course, it has to be a dog with the appropriate temperament to put up with this exercise.) Then, work the sheep to the mouth of the pen and see how close you can come to penning them against this counter-force. When I explain this to my students, they complain: "But we'll never get the sheep in under those conditions!" That may be true. However, this exercise will help them learn to get the sheep to the mouth of the pen, against strong counter-pressures and to be alert to the sheep's strong flight instincts. Penning is not accomplished by shutting the gate; it is accomplished by getting the sheep to the mouth of the pen and then applying pressure without allowing the sheep to get away. This type of exercise will truly test the penning teamwork of you and your dog.

When penning at home, never allow a young dog to bring the sheep out of the pen. The dog's natural instinct will be to run to the back

♠ FROM THE HANDLER'S POST ♠

of the pen in order to block the perceived escape of the sheep. If you allow your dog to go to the back of the pen, you are reinforcing this instinct. And invariably, at a trial the dog will anticipate that command and slip around to the back of the pen before you have the gate closed! Therefore, when you are training your dog, have him pen the sheep, and then walk him up to the gate opening, to demonstrate to him that you and he have accomplished the desired task and that the sheep are not escaping. Then, walk the dog away from the pen and lie him down. Go back and get the sheep out of the pen yourself; then allow the dog to catch the sheep and continue your training session. Even if you are at a trial, I recommend that you follow this procedure, so that your dog does not acquire bad habits. Otherwise, this will come back to haunt you!

    Another training hint is to pen the sheep, turn your pen 45 degrees, and try it again; turn the pen another 45 degrees and pen once more. Continue this exercise until you have made a complete circle, and study how the pressures and the responses of the sheep vary with each angle and each approach. You will see that some angles make the pen look easy and the sheep look broke; other angles will be nearly impossible.

Finally, as we have stated before: remember that practice does not make perfect; rather, *perfect* practice makes perfect. You need to practice not only the pen itself, but also the set-up to the pen. Practice the line from the crossdrive panels to the pen; if you do not bring the sheep directly to the mouth of the pen, take them back to the crossdrive panels and try it again. If something goes wrong, try once more. Fix the problem at the point where it goes wrong, until both you and your dog have mended the hole in your teamwork. Remember that the successful run at a trial is the one in which each segment is perfect, and the only way to achieve this is to work on "nuts and bolts" at home. In this way, you and your dog will have the right tools at your disposal to handle the unexpected situations that can arise at the pen.

9

The Shed

> *One sheep is to be shed off and held to the satisfaction of the judge. The shed must be done within the ring by the dog and not the handler, and the judge must be satisfied that the dog has proved its ability to "hold" the single before he or she shall indicate satisfaction.*
> *—10 points*

Shedding is one of the most sophisticated and complex tasks that takes place on the trial course. While both attentive stockmanship and teamwork are necessary throughout your run, these elements are really put to the test in the shedding ring. In addition, perhaps more than in any other segment of the course, shedding requires that your dog truly understand the job to be done.

As you set up for the shed, the dog needs to know what you expect to happen next. He needs to participate actively in the setting up of the shed, hold himself back from the sheep until called in, and once called, he must move quickly and with authority, holding the indicated sheep away from the others without becoming excited or over-anxious. The handler must also understand the task, rather than hoping for luck or for sheep that don't want to stay together.

Complicating this delicate balance is the fact that shedding requires handler, dog, and sheep to work in close proximity, which can make the sheep feel trapped and can make the dog more anxious. Also, the handler is often working against a time element, either because this is the last segment of the course, or because he knows he needs to leave enough time for the pen. And finally, the shed often occurs in close proximity to the exhaust pen, creating additional tension because of the sheep's pressure to move in that direction.

To mitigate all of these stress factors, the handler should enter the shedding ring with a plan, and then work calmly and methodically—and have the dog work calmly and in a workmanlike fashion as well—to make that plan

♠ FROM THE HANDLER'S POST ♠

happen. For purposes of this discussion, we shall assume that the shed takes place immediately following the drive and before the pen; we shall also assume, as is the general practice, that the handler was asked to "take the last sheep on the head."

As the sheep make (or miss) the crossdrive panel, the handler should begin to set up the shed by drawing an imaginary line from the outside edge of the crossdrive panel to the center of the shedding ring (a circle generally measuring 40 yards in diameter). On the third leg of the drive, pace and line can be crucial to a successful shed. In terms of line, if the handler relaxes his guard—as often happens during this part of the course—the agenda of the sheep may take over, and the sheep begin to feel somewhat more free to make their own decisions; however, eventually the dog will have to regain control, and this is likely to worry the sheep. Often, sheep will drift toward the exhaust point (or other pressure point), and the dog will then have to be flanked to divert them. All of these actions work against your chances for a clean and successful shed on the first attempt. Pace, on the third leg of the drive, is perhaps even more important to a handler who wants a perfect shed. The sheep, ideally, should *walk* into the shedding ring. The handler should not need to jump in front of them, or wave his crook, or flank his dog hard, or need other drastic maneuvers to slow them down at the end of the drive.

As a general rule, once the sheep enter the ring, the handler may leave the post and approach the sheep. Already, from those first steps he takes toward the sheep, the handler should begin to apply practiced strategies and techniques to set up the perfect shed. The faster and more efficiently the set-up can be accomplished, the greater are the chances for a ten-point shed.

The handler should plan to use the dog a great deal during the set-up, rather than attempting to do the work himself. This is not only because the judge can deduct points for the handler doing more than he ought, but also because the dog has greater and steadier control over the sheep than a person does.

The perfect "set-up" involves getting all of the sheep to walk, in a line, across the shedding ring. In order to accomplish this, as mentioned above, the sheep should be calm when they enter the ring. If the handler does need to act to slow down or stop the sheep, he should do so in as unobtrusive a manner as possible, perhaps with body position or with very slight movements of the crook.

Short flanks by the dog, and some movement by the handler, should create a space between

♠ FROM THE HANDLER'S POST ♠

the last and the second-to-last sheep in the line. Strategies for achieving this will be discussed later in this section. Once the hole is created and the dog has been called in, the dog should move in quickly and with a good attitude, focusing immediately on the single sheep and not even glancing back toward the others.

If the dog doesn't come in all the way to the middle—that is, to an imaginary line between the single sheep and the others—but he clearly has taken charge and keeps the single sheep from attempting to rejoin the others, this should still be a ten-point shed, because the pressures may be such that, if the dog were to move all the way to the middle, he would in fact create an escape route on one side or the other. The dog, and perhaps the handler, are in a better position to determine the shed's "balance point" than is the judge, and for this reason judges should be very careful about docking points for a dog not coming "all the way through," if in fact the single sheep is under complete control.

For the ideal shed, that single sheep will still be looking at the dog when the dog comes in; that last sheep will not already have turned around and be walking in the opposite direction when the handler calls the dog in. As we shall discuss, competitive handlers who are focusing on the perfect run—barring time pressures, erratic sheep, etc.—will not take the shed that occurs in this accidental fashion. Rather, they will regroup the sheep and set up the shed again, attempting to take the last sheep "on the head."

Most judges specify that the dog should hold the sheep until the judge indicates that he is satisfied. Judges should be cautious about asking the dog to hold the single sheep too long, because this can force a grip. Once the judge is certain that the dog has taken charge, he should promptly call that a successful shed. If the judge leaves it to the handler's discretion to determine how long the dog should hold that single sheep, the handler should call the dog off quickly, once he has taken charge.

Finally, after the shed has been completed, the handler must re-group the sheep in the shedding ring before proceeding to the pen. This also requires some advance planning, in terms of setting up the shed in such a way that the lead sheep are less likely to bolt toward the exhaust pen and thus be more difficult to recover later. Ideally, the lead sheep would simply walk away and would never even leave the ring. Sheep can then easily be re-gathered and the handler can proceed to the next phase of work.

The shed described above, the one we all strive to achieve in every Open competition, is ideal for several reasons. First, it is accom-

♠ FROM THE HANDLER'S POST ♠

plished in a minimal amount of time, leaving more time for the pen. Second, it is performed with minimal upset to the sheep, who will then be less likely to bolt for the exhaust and will be calmer at the pen. Third, a shed as we have described costs minimal physical effort on the part of the dog, who has just run a very strenuous trial course and still needs some energy for the pen. Finally, based on standards of real work, the task as outlined above is efficient and workmanlike. For all of these reasons, a judge should only award the full ten points if he has really seen the "perfect shed."

Handlers who are relatively new to Open competition are often so elated by the fact that they "got" the shed that they forget all of the errors that occurred in the process; they are then shocked by the scores that they receive. Competitive stockdog trialing requires that handlers not only complete each phase, but do so with a minimum of points deducted, and the close work—penning and shedding—often marks the difference between first and tenth place. When practicing and during competition, handlers should be alert to the following common errors for which most judges will deduct points.

One element of judging with which handlers might not be familiar is the fact that, during the shed (and the pen), some errors do not cost a specific number of points, but rather "half of the remaining points." Thus, an error that costs one handler five points might cost another handler only two or three points, if that handler has already lost significant points during other parts of the shed (for example, from earlier missed attempts). The judge has ten points to work with, and the shed is sometimes a lengthy process involving several separate errors or critical moments. For these reasons it is impossible to assign a set number of points to each of the errors that might occur. It is even possible for a handler to lose all ten of his points, but still complete the shed and be permitted to move on to the next phase of work.

The judge expects that the dog will do the majority of work during the set-up process. Handlers who lie the dog down and then proceed to move back and forth themselves, using the crook or their own body language to attempt to create a gap, will lose points for not effectively using the dog. Furthermore, once the hole is created, the handler must step back and call the dog into the space. If the handler steps forward into the space, or steps toward the sheep at all, the judge will probably deduct points.

The most common loss of points occurs when the handler calls the dog in, but either the dog does not come in quickly enough or the hole closes up, causing a missed shed. This results in

♠ FROM THE HANDLER'S POST ♠

a loss of at least three points per missed attempt.

If a hole is made and, in the judge's opinion, the handler should have called the dog in but did not, this is termed a "missed opportunity" and will result in a loss of one or two points. However, judges should be cautious about taking this deduction, since it may be that the dog was slightly out of position or other factors were in play that made the opportunity too risky or made the handler uncertain of his success.

If the sheep step out of the shedding ring at any point, the judge will deduct points. As a general rule, the judge deducts one point per sheep that leaves the ring. For this reason, handlers should attempt to set up the shed as close to the middle of the ring as possible and to keep the sheep calm and settled.

Points may also be lost if, in the opinion of the judge, the handler does not proceed in a workmanlike fashion and takes too long in the set-up process. If the dog comes in too slowly (and if the sheep are kind enough not to close the hole in the meantime), and it appears that the handler needs to "beg" the dog to come in, the judge may take off points. The dog should come in sharply and with a good attitude. Furthermore, if the dog charges toward the sheep in what looks like an attempted grip, the judge may take a deduction of points.

"Switching sides" is a common source of point deductions during the shed. Once you have set up the shed, with you on one side and the dog on the other, you should maintain those positions. You may rotate in a circle, keeping the sheep between you; but you and your dog should not "cross" to opposite sides; generally, this only occurs when the sheep split and manage to move around behind you. Because of the loss of points that this can cause, you should be prepared either to back away from the sheep or to flank your dog in order to prevent this.

For full points, it is essential that your dog not turn toward the sheep that are leaving; in fact, your dog should not even glance in their direction. His full attention should be on the sheep that is being held. It does not matter where the handler is facing, in terms of points—I have seen cases where the handler got flustered and turned toward the wrong sheep, but the dog, knowing his job, kept his attention on the single sheep. There would be no deduction of points for this. However, it is important for the handler to realize that the dog takes cues from him. The handler should therefore also be facing the single sheep and indicating to the dog that that is the sheep he is intended to hold.

The concept of the "last sheep" causes some confusion among newer handlers. Every group of

♠ FROM THE HANDLER'S POST ♠

sheep has a "lead sheep" and a "last sheep," but this designation is changing constantly according to the circumstances of the moment. If the lead sheep suddenly feels at risk and ducks back behind another one, then that is no longer the lead sheep. If the last sheep panics and bolts forward, then probably that individual is no longer the last sheep. If the entire group of sheep suddenly turns around, then the lead sheep suddenly becomes the last sheep! Handlers should be very alert and use all of their stockmanship skills in order to take advantage of changing dynamics. During the set-up and call-in of the shed, many events may occur regarding the last sheep that can result in a loss of points.

For example, if the last sheep turns to walk away from the others before the handler has called the dog in, and the handler calls the dog in anyway, the judge might call the shed complete, but he might deduct half of the remaining shed points.

Sometimes the lead sheep will walk away, and the handler, uncertain of future possibilities, will call the dog in on that sheep. Most judges would call that a complete shed, but would deduct most of the points from that shed. As a strategy, then, this should only be done if the handler feels that other options are impossible, and he is therefore willing to sacrifice the points in order to move on to the pen or to "take what he can get." Such strategies generally do not result in a winning run.

Failing to re-group the sheep in the shedding ring before proceeding to the pen also costs points, but these points are deducted from the pen rather than from the shed. Once the dog is holding the single sheep away from the others and the judge has indicated his satisfaction, the shed portion of the course is complete and no further points should be deducted.

The best chance for a ten-point shed occurs immediately after the sheep enter the shedding ring. As we described in detail earlier, the ideal shed involves the sheep walking into the ring in a straight line, the handler walking toward the sheep, two or three sheep calmly walking away, one sheep lagging behind, the dog coming in sharply and authoritatively as the handler backs away, and the judge indicating that the shed is complete. But how can we make this happen?

Shedding requires that the handler have a plan. While the circumstances of the shedding ring change constantly, the plan itself should not change. Instead, the plan should allow for varying circumstances, so that the handler is not caught off guard no matter what happens. A plan is developed through careful and extensive practice. The plan should involve several stages: how to bring the sheep into the ring, how the

♠ FROM THE HANDLER'S POST ♠

handler approaches the sheep, assessing the dynamics within the group of sheep, setting up the shed via movements of the dog and the handler, calling in the dog, and holding the single sheep (or two sheep) away from the others. A good shedding plan also involves having taught your dog to understand the task at hand. The dog should realize, as soon as you leave the post, that he is about to set up for a shed. He should be watchful for your body language and commands, ready to flank in either direction, and ready to come in when called. Handler-dog teams that are comfortable with their plan, and who use it automatically and easily rather than relying on luck or hoping for the best, are far more likely to accomplish the ideal shed.

The perfect shed begins with the sheep's approach to the shedding ring. Many handlers breathe a sigh of relief when they round the last corner of the drive, and they let down their guard. In their minds they might be thinking about the set-up for the shed, but they are only thinking about what happens after the sheep enter the shedding ring. They do not realize that the last leg of the drive has a great deal to do with the mindset of the sheep during the shed.

The third leg of the drive, the portion to which handlers pay the least attention, is in fact often the most difficult portion of the course in terms of maintaining a straight line, because frequently the last leg of the drive involves bringing the sheep past the exhaust pen or some other pressure point. If the sheep have been allowed to drift off course, then their agenda has taken priority. Forcing the dog to resume control and change their course can make the sheep anxious, which will make them more difficult to shed. Equally important is the issue of pace on the last leg of the drive. Sheep that run pell-mell into the shedding ring will certainly be more difficult to shed than sheep which walk into the ring. Therefore, the handler should be actively preparing for a successful shed from the time that the sheep turn the last corner of the drive.

The next element to which handlers often do not pay attention is their own approach to the sheep. Generally the handler can leave the post as the sheep cross into the shedding ring. At this point, many handlers walk directly toward the sheep. If possible, this should be avoided. When the handler walks into the shedding ring, he should be aware that he needs to leave an "opening," a place toward which the sheep feel like they can go. If the handler brings the sheep to a complete stop, then somehow he must start them moving again; this requires startling or worrying them to some extent. Also, bringing them to a complete stop can encourage them

♠ FROM THE HANDLER'S POST ♠

to group together more tightly, thus making the shed more difficult. For these reasons, the handler should not walk directly toward the heads of the sheep, but rather should approach them from an angle.

As the handler approaches the sheep, he can influence their direction with careful and subtle movements of the crook. At this point, the handler should be assessing how close he should get to the sheep, based on how people-shy or people-friendly they are. If the shed occurs before the pen, then this is the first time the handler is really working in close proximity to the stock. In a sense, the handler must do what the dog did earlier, during the initial lift—establish a relationship with the sheep, perceive the distance at which he should work in order to influence movement without startling the stock. If the sheep are overly people-shy, the handler should keep himself at quite a distance from them. Equally, if the sheep are overly people-friendly, the handler should stay back, in order to prevent the sheep from clinging to him or darting around him. These assessments come from experience with many different types of sheep, and from attention to the sheep's reactions as he approaches.

If the handler notices that the sheep are becoming worried by his approach, he should not be afraid to back away and relieve the pressure.

We all teach our dogs to do this; we also need to have a "go-back" command for ourselves, in order to maintain a calm demeanor in the sheep and not push them toward the dog, where they would become uncomfortable.

During this approach, then, the handler should not already be hoping for a hole but should be settling the sheep and assessing the right strategy for creating the hole. The next phase involves looking for the "weak link in the chain." This means identifying which sheep are probably too nervous to be shed off from the others, which one might be an obvious leader, etc. One key to a successful set-up is small movements on the part of the dog. Ideally, throughout the shed you would never need to swing the dog all the way around to the heads of the sheep. Rather, small flanks would slow down the leader, create some hesitation in the follower, encourage forward movement without bolting, and establish just the right "escape route" for the lead sheep. The dog should be able to take one or two steps in each direction without ever decreasing his distance from the sheep, in order to influence their movement without applying too much pressure.

Another critical element is the distance at which the dog should work from the sheep. If the dog is too far away, the sheep will feel that they should attempt an escape. But if the dog is

♠ FROM THE HANDLER'S POST ♠

too close, the sheep will be insecure about separating from each other. The right spot for the dog is far enough away that the leader feels comfortable in walking away rather than turning toward the handler or bolting, but close enough that the rear sheep hesitate. Forward-to-back positioning is every bit as essential as left-to-right positioning. In this regard, the well-trained shedding dog will already know at what distance he should work. He has had an entire trial course during which he has established his relationship to the sheep and his authority, and if he has done so in a quiet and controlled manner, the payoff will come in the shedding ring.

The moment when the hole starts to open up between the lead sheep and the rear one is the time to move your dog into the exact position for the shed. You should not leave your dog stationary at this moment, hoping that the last sheep does not change his mind. Instead you should be pro-active and give that one final command which will cause the last sheep to stand and look at your dog.

The correct position is never at a 90-degree angle from that last sheep. This is a common error that handlers make, placing the dog perpendicular to the imaginary line between the last sheep and the others. In fact, your dog should be at an angle that places him in *front* of that last sheep.

If the dog is slightly behind the last sheep, he will cause that sheep to bolt forward as he comes in, increasing the chances of either a miss or a grip. If the dog is at a 90-degree angle to that sheep, he is still quite likely to grip, because of the possibility of that sheep moving forward at the last instant. However, if the dog is positioned slightly in front of that last sheep, the shed is almost guaranteed to happen, because that sheep will stop and stare, and know that he will not be able to beat the dog. This positioning is an essential element for a successful shed.

Equally important is the spot where the handler should stand: at this moment. In your mind, you should imagine you and your dog as a chute through which the sheep are intended to walk, and your decision is where you will close the cutting gate. Like the dog, you should not be in a position perpendicular to the chute. Instead, you should be slightly in front of the sheep—perhaps even farther in front of the last sheep than your dog needs to be, because the sheep are somewhat less intimidated by you than they are by the dog.

When the handler calls the dog in, it is essential that the handler not move forward but rather actively move backward, allowing the dog

♠ FROM THE HANDLER'S POST ♠

to make the "cut." The handler needs to get out of the way and leave enough room that the dog can flank in either direction, as needed, to stop the sheep. The handler should be facing the last sheep, in order to indicate the sheep over which the dog is intended to take charge. And finally, if possible, the handler should be in such a position that he can keep the dog in his field of vision. That way, if the dog should start to tense up and a grip becomes likely, the handler can take the dog off his feet quickly and restore calm, even if that results in a missed shed.

An awareness of how to use field pressures to one's own advantage is a critical aspect of all phases of the trial, and it is of particular importance during the shed. Well in advance of the handler's own entrance to the shedding ring, he should already be aware of where the pressures lie, and how strongly they influence the movement of the sheep. In general, the handler should never be the one who guards the pressure side. In other words, as the sheep enter the shedding ring, the handler should move away from the pressure side of the ring and move the dog toward the pressure side.

If the pressure is quite strong, then the sheep should not be lined up such that they would be invited to move directly toward the pressure (e.g. the exhaust pen). There are two reasons why this would be dangerous. The first is that the last sheep is less likely to be willing to be left behind as the front sheep move toward the exhaust gate. The second reason is that, if the front sheep bolt toward the "escape chute," they will be more difficult to retrieve when it is time to re-group them.

Nonetheless, the pressure can be a useful draw in terms of easing the sheep apart. Therefore, the sheep should be lined up at an oblique angle to the pressure, such that the lead sheep are invited to walk in that general direction, but not directly on the imaginary line between sheep and pressure point.

Because of the potential usefulness of this dynamic, after a missed attempt it might be best for the handler to line the sheep up again in the same relationship to the pressure point, even if this means making a full circle before beginning the second set-up. Handlers should be very cautious about this too, however, since full circles both tire the dog and worry the sheep, with the additional risk factors that the dog might widen out too far or slice in too closely. It is far better to flank early and often, in whatever directions might be necessary, in order to turn sheep around rather than make a wide, full circle.

Once the sheep have been lined up in correct relationship to the pressure, if the dog is slightly in front of the last sheep—causing it to hesi-

♠ FROM THE HANDLER'S POST ♠

tate—and the handler is also out in front of that sheep, then the dog should be called in. At this point, the correct and accurate movement of the handler is important. If the sheep are very people-oriented, then it can create a problem if the handler backs straight away as the dog comes in. This can draw the sheep toward the person, which is in effect a forward motion, since the handler was positioned out in front of the sheep's head. To compensate for this tendency, it may be necessary for the handler to move away and back—toward the rear of the sheep. This will increase the sheep's sense of hesitation as it is drawn slightly away from the dog and toward the handler and is less likely to try to bolt forward. Handlers should try to visualize this as a drawing of the type that football coaches use to demonstrate a play, because these directional movements are difficult to describe in words. The handler should realize that, if the sheep are people-oriented, his own direction of movement can be used to advantage during this critical moment of the shed. The handler should back up not in a direction perpendicular to the "escape chute," but rather at an angle toward the rear of the sheep.

    Another strategy that is helpful, particularly with younger dogs, is to warn them just before the call-in. At the moment when the lead sheep are walking away, the dog almost inevitably has at least part of his attention on them, hoping that he will be asked to re-group them. For this reason, as I see the hole opening up, I will often say the dog's name, quietly but firmly. This returns the dog's attention to me and alerts him to the fact that his attention should be on the last sheep rather than the departing sheep. This can be a very effective tactic for keeping the dog focused on the task at hand.

The way that the handler issues the call-in command is very important. First and foremost, the handler should never use "that'll do" as the call-in command. Instead, there should be a particular command that means "come in and take control" rather than "come toward me." Many trainers use "come in," or "in here," uttered in an authoritative tone. Some trainers then add another command, such as "this one" or "these," to indicate which sheep should be held. Handlers should be aware of the effect that their tone of voice has on the dog's manner. If the handler speaks with too much urgency or nervousness, the dog is likely to blow in too quickly. This creates the risk not only of panicking the last sheep, but also of sending the lead sheep away too quickly, thus making re-grouping more difficult. The dog, as he comes in, should take charge, but should not startle either the last sheep or the departing sheep. As

♠ FROM THE HANDLER'S POST ♠

mentioned previously, ideally the lead sheep would never even feel it necessary to leave the shedding ring.

Once the hole begins to open up, often the last sheep will turn around and walk away. This is a "strategy moment" for the competitive handler. If the dog has already been called in before the sheep turns, there would not be a major deduction of points—perhaps only one point—and the handler should proceed with the shed. However, if the sheep turns around before the dog has been called in, the handler should assess how well the rest of the run has gone, how much time remains, and how much time might be needed for the pen. If the handler has enough time, and the rest of the run has gone very well, the best competitive strategy is to resist the temptation, re-group the sheep, and begin again. This is the only way to accomplish a ten-point shed. However, if time is short and starting over would make it unlikely that the pen would be accomplished, or if the shed is the last element of the course and "some points are better than none," or if the dog is simply too tired to be able to set up a better situation the next time, then the handler should go ahead and take that shed, hoping that the judge will be kind.

Strategy is important at every stage of the trialing game, including how the sheep are regrouped after the shed and before the pen. Often, the lead sheep will have moved off toward the exhaust area, and frequently, the pen is placed in the same direction. If this is the case, then as the dog is retrieving the sheep, the handler should be thinking about how best to set up the situation. As the dog is bringing back the sheep, he is likely to be right on the "pressure line," and he might then be forced to make a 180-degree flank in order to move the sheep toward the pen. This long and wide flank will open up the escape chute again, sending the sheep toward the exhaust rather than toward the pen. The handler should anticipate this problem and keep the dog as far off the sheep as possible, so that a very short flank will ease the sheep into motion again, and in the precise direction that the handler needs them to go.

The solidity of the handler's training program becomes apparent in the shedding ring. The quality of the handler's run at a trial is largely based on how carefully the training was done at home. There is a very precise way in which dogs should be trained to shed, in progressive stages, such that the dog learns his job, recognizes the signals, and automatically avoids potential problem situations.

Teaching the shed begins in the very first lessons of the training program. The first step in teaching a shed is simply lying the dog down,

♠ FROM THE HANDLER'S POST ♠

moving through the flock yourself, calling the dog to you, and rewarding him for putting his attention on you rather than on the sheep. This teaches the dog to move toward the sheep and toward you, with his attention on you rather than on "catching sheep."

The point at which teaching the shed should advance to the next phase—splitting the sheep into two groups—depends on the dog. If a dog is quite strong-eyed, and very conscious of the need to keep sheep together, then teaching the shed should begin early, within the first month or two of training. This will allow the dog to learn that keeping the sheep together is not always the first priority.

In contrast, if a dog is somewhat loose-eyed or sloppy and doesn't seem to mind if some sheep walk away, then teaching the shed should be delayed somewhat. Instead, those dogs should be given time to mature, to develop more eye and to become more secure about their job.

Once you do begin to teach the dog to split sheep, it is best to use a large group, perhaps between thirty and sixty sheep if possible. When you first begin, you should stop the dog, allow a hole to appear (at this stage you should not be afraid to make the hole yourself), and then call the dog to you. By the third or fourth time that you practice this exercise, you should also be able to turn the dog's attention to the group of sheep you want.

If the dog is not yet proficient at flanks, or has not yet become comfortable with driving, then you should not be afraid to go around to the front of the sheep you have chosen for him to hold and allow him to wear one group of sheep away from the other. This will teach him to guard the space and keep the two groups from getting back together, and eventually the rest of his training program will "catch up" to the point that he will be able to drive one group away from the other.

Once the dog understands the concept of coming through the sheep, you should begin to teach the set-up. This is the point where you are really teaching the idea of shedding, allowing the dog to gain an understanding of the overall task. It should be remembered that setting up the shed is in fact much more important and much more difficult than accomplishing the shed itself. For this reason, you should devote extensive time to teaching your dog to work one side of the flock while you work the other, setting up a hole through which the dog can be called. In teaching the set-up, it doesn't even matter if you call the dog in; teaching the dog to help you create the hole is the essential element of this stage of training.

♠ FROM THE HANDLER'S POST ♠

Because the dog has been bred and trained to hold sheep to you, it can be very difficult at first for the dog to flank in the same direction you are walking—for example, moving in a "come-bye" direction while you are also moving from left-to-right. The dog's natural tendency would be to flank in the opposite direction. Anticipating this, you should be prepared to help your dog by having your crook in the correct hand, indicating to him that you need him to flank toward the sheep's heads in spite of the fact that you are also heading in that direction. Teach short flanks, in each direction; teach the dog to follow your directions rather than to work based exclusively on where the leaders of the flock are going.

One exercise which is both fun and useful is to take a large group of sheep and split them in half, then move away with one half of them, and split them again, allowing the leaders to rejoin the rest of the flock. Then split the smaller group, and continue until you are holding about five sheep. Until the dog is comfortable with the task, you should not split the group into any fewer than five sheep; eventually, when the dog is ready, you can reduce the group to one single sheep. This exercise allows you to create different pressures in your field, and it also gives your leaders somewhere to go, more closely mimicking a trial situation.

An essential element of this phase of training is resisting the temptation to take the "lucky" shed. If a hole opens up, but you and your dog did not create the hole, then you should *not* call your dog in. Let the hole close up, and begin again. Neither you nor your dog will learn anything from luck, and luck is not something that is in great supply at the trial field. Instead, you and your dog will learn more from setting up a shed carefully, creating a situation, and seeing it materialize. At home, you do not have the pressures of a time clock, and you should fully avail yourself of this opportunity to improve your stockmanship skills and extend your dog's patience, so that you both have the necessary mileage and skills once you do get to the trial shedding ring.

10

The International Shed

The philosophy of the ideal international shed is to accomplish the task with as little movement as possible on the part of the stock, the dog, and the handler. Of paramount importance for this goal is that the stock remain settled and relaxed. Any sheep, once alarmed, will cluster together, or will attempt to bolt past or over a dog, thus making the task at hand nearly impossible. But if the dog maintains his distance and avoids startling movements, if the handler maintains his calm demeanor and tries not to let certain sheep feel "marked," and if the sheep are not made to feel threatened in any way, then the task can be accomplished beautifully and efficiently.

First, an explanation of the precise task might be helpful to the handler who may have watched an international shed but might not understand the underlying strategies or mechanisms. The standard international shed involves twenty sheep, five of which have been selected at random and fitted with clearly visible collars. In a standard shed (the splitting off of the last one or two sheep), the handler and the dog make a "hole" or a space, and then the dog moves into that space, facing the "held" sheep and preventing them from re-grouping. In the international shed, on the other hand, the emphasis is on allowing sheep to escape. The handler and the dog form an imaginary gate, which they alternately open and close, allowing the unmarked sheep (generally the sheep without collars) to drift away a few at a time, until finally only the collared sheep remain in the ring.

As with the standard shed, an important and often overlooked element to remember is that the calm atmosphere of the shed is in fact established much earlier, throughout the course and particularly toward the end of the drive. When pressed for time or when stressed, handlers often neglect to exercise the precision that is necessary during the final leg of the drive; they bring the sheep too quickly, allow the dog to apply too much pressure, and then find themselves having to wave a crook or flank the dog in order to stop the sheep once they get to the ring. Successful trialers start planning for

♠ FROM THE HANDLER'S POST ♠

the international shed as the sheep approach the ring, not after they get there.

The handler may leave the post as soon as the sheep enter the shedding ring. He should endeavor always to work toward the center of the ring, to give himself enough room to maneuver and to minimize the chance that any sheep will step out of the ring.

In terms of points as well as efficiency, two elements are of crucial importance. One is that the handler and the dog avoid "switching sides." The handler should imagine a working chute between him and his dog. This chute is the pathway through which certain sheep will be permitted to "escape." Switching sides involves the handler and/or the dog crossing through this pathway, thus alarming or upsetting the sheep and minimizing the chance for the perfect shed. Because this kind of crossing over demonstrates a lack of precision and the lack of a plan for accomplishing the shed, judges deduct points liberally for this error.

The second major deduction occurs when sheep step out of the ring. As in all phases of stockdog trialing, the task of the international shed is designed with the practicalities of farm work in mind. Stockmen who need a wider working area for the sorting task obviously are less efficient, tire their dogs more quickly, and put more stress on their stock. Therefore, the ideal international shed occurs toward the center of the ring, and with a minimum of "travel" on the part of the sheep and the dog. As a final consideration, during trialing the handler must consider that the international shed is generally not the final task of the competition; the job of penning still lies ahead, and the dog needs to have enough energy left for that element of the course.

Time is also an important consideration, for the reasons mentioned above. In terms of farm work, a task completed more quickly leaves more time for the other endless jobs that must be done. In terms of the trial course, an efficient shed leaves more time for penning. Therefore, successful handlers check their watches at the beginning of the shed and stay aware of how much time has passed. This being said, however, it should also be stressed that the international shed is not a phase of work that can be rushed. Often, handlers look at their watches not so that they will hurry, but in order to calm themselves, to assure themselves that they have enough time to proceed deliberately and with a quiet demeanor. (This is a good trialing hint not only for the international shed, but for the standard shed and for penning as well; the psychological aspect of trialing is often as important as the physical aspect.)

♠ FROM THE HANDLER'S POST ♠

Prior to beginning the international shed, the handler should have studied the field and its pressures in order to decide in what direction he will set up his imaginary work chute. One item of trialing advice that has been repeated throughout this book is the importance of studying the field in advance of one's run. Field pressures can be used to great advantage during the international shed, and ignoring those pressures can make the shed much more difficult or even impossible. If the handler drives some sheep in a direction contrary to the pressure, then that group of sheep might later drift toward the pressure point, and thus across the path that you are trying to create. Generally, by the final day of a trial, the field's strongest pressure is toward the exhaust pen. If this is the case, then the imaginary chute should be aimed in that general direction. However, the handler should study whether the pressure is too strong in that direction; this would cause the remaining sheep to be more difficult to hold as they watch their fellow flock members drift in that direction. Juggling these delicate pressures, creating a magnet that pulls strongly enough but not too strongly, is a key to the successful international shed.

Once the handler is physically and psychologically set up near the center of the ring, with himself and his dog as the two sides of the chute, he should pause for one more moment that can prove crucial—he should identify and count the collared sheep. This is an item that is often overlooked, but it can save a lot of time or even cause a re-run. It is not infrequent that one sheep loses a collar somewhere on the course, or an error can be made and only four sheep collared. Furthermore, collars are sometimes difficult to see on woolly sheep. Handlers will avoid problems by counting the collared sheep not only at this point, but with some frequency throughout the shed. I have seen many sheds during which a collared sheep sneaks past the handler, hiding his collared neck behind another sheep, and the handler wastes precious minutes continuing the shed without realizing that he only has four collared sheep remaining! Counting the collared sheep, then, should become an automatic part of the international shed.

Finally, with all of these early preparations completed, the handler should begin to plan the first "cut." The goal of the handler at this point is to take as many uncollared sheep as possible. One reason for this is obvious—so that fewer sheep remain to be sorted. But the other, less obvious reason is that a fairly large group of sheep is more likely to stay put once it has been driven out of the ring. As a new source of pressure, the sheep that have been driven away

♠ FROM THE HANDLER'S POST ♠

will, ideally, stop and graze, serving as a magnet for the next sort of sheep. In order to function effectively as a magnet, they must be nearby, but not so close that the remaining sheep are too powerfully drawn in that direction, and not so close that, should a collared sheep bolt, the dog does not have time or space to catch it.

The handler needs to take his time at this point; subtle moves are the key to this early maneuvering. It is important not to stir up the sheep. As long as the sheep are more or less stationary, the dog is not asked to move much. He should be stationed toward the front of the flock, holding the pressure somewhat, but not so much that the sheep turn and go the other way. The flock should always be looking in the direction that you want them to go. Also, remember that the dog's distance from the sheep is crucial; he should be near enough to apply pressure, but not so close that he is pushing the sheep toward the handler (at this level of trialing, sheep tend to be quite wary of people and will grow nervous if pushed). After positioning the dog, the handler takes the time for the "assessment" phase of this task; he moves back and forth, studying the behavior of the collared sheep, identifying leaders and attempting to discourage any collared sheep that appear too anxious to lead. In a very subtle way, the handler attempts to work collared sheep toward the back of the flock, and uncollared sheep toward the front. The dog should be moved as necessary, but hopefully only in small increments. For this task, it is important that the dog be very fluid, easy to move in either direction, and that he automatically maintains his distance off the sheep.

In contrast to the traditional shed, it is the handler who performs the sorting of the uncollared sheep for the international shed. In the traditional shed, the handler steps back and pulls the dog into the space that has been created. But for the international shed, the dog holds the rear sheep, while the handler steps in and, as quietly as possible, drives the first cut of sheep out of the ring. Because this is so different from the way most dogs have been trained, it is important that your dog understand the task at hand—more than once, as handlers have been focused on driving sheep away, dogs have circled around to bring the trailing sheep to the handler, and that can certainly create an unpleasant surprise. As the handler drives the sheep away, it may be necessary to call the dog in a step or two, to hold the sheep firmly in place (ideally without turning their heads).

The handler then returns to his own side of the sheep, re-positions the dog, and begins to work on the second sort. In evaluating the shed, the judge does not consider how many sorts are

♠ FROM THE HANDLER'S POST ♠

necessary. If the task is accomplished smoothly and correctly, the handler who accomplishes the shed in only two or three sorts does not have more points than the handler who uses more sorts. Thus, sheep can be allowed to escape two or three at a time, rather than in large groups, and this may be easier to accomplish. With each sort, the handler may have to step in and drive uncollared sheep away, while the dog maintains control over the collared sheep.

We are describing here the ideal shed; the next section will cover eventualities that can occur and strategies for managing those cases. But in the ideal shed, the dog never has to leave the group of "held" sheep. This also allows for valuable rest and recuperation time for the dog, after what has probably been an arduous course involving a double lift and a long drive; a lot of dashing and catching during the international shed can really use up a dog's remaining stamina, not only costing points later but endangering the dog's health. Thus, having an effective plan and an arsenal of strategies is crucial for the successful international shed.

Finally, a situation that should be avoided is ending up with six sheep, five collared and one uncollared. It can be extremely difficult to convince this last sheep to leave the flock to which it has become increasingly attached. Thus, in the ideal international shed, the last sort involves at least two or three sheep. Of course, this cannot always be accomplished, and later we will discuss what to do if that situation should arise.

Once the handler and dog are left with the five uncollared sheep, the handler leaves the dog with the sheep and proceeds to the pen; once he opens the gate of the pen, he then asks the dog to bring the sheep and completes the final phase of work.

We have presented the ideal international shed, the one we all dream about and would like to accomplish each time we compete. However, ideal sheds are extremely rare, and it is much more important to know what situations to avoid and how to make the best of them if they should occur. I will review some of the ways that points can be deducted, but handlers should remember the general philosophy of stockdog trialing: for full points, the task must be accomplished with maximum efficiency and with minimal stress (physical or mental) to the stock.

Each time that any marked sheep step out of the shedding ring, points may be deducted. If the handler and the dog switch sides (thus crossing through their imaginary "work chute"), the judge will take points.

Once the sheep have been parted into two groups, several pitfalls can cause the deduction

♠ FROM THE HANDLER'S POST ♠

of points. If the handler steps into the hole but cannot drive the sheep away—if they fold around him or fail to move off in the indicated direction—this will result in a loss of points. Also, if the dog is brought too far into the hole, thus crossing into the handler's side of the imaginary chute, points can be deducted. Likewise, the handler should avoid crossing into the dog's side of the chute; this will also result in a loss of points.

I have discussed the importance of the initial assessment phase during the international shed. However, if the handler spends too much time playing, walking back and forth, points can be deducted for "failure to progress." Again, farm work standards are applied; efficiency is important, and the task should be accomplished in a workmanlike manner.

Most of us do not often—if ever—experience the ideal international shed. Instead of just hoping for that, competitive handlers prepare for the other eventualities and can respond automatically if the unexpected occurs. If a collared sheep does escape from the ring, the dog should immediately be sent to catch it. If that collared sheep leaves the ring, some points will be lost, but if the dog can retrieve it quickly, far fewer points will be lost than if the worst-case scenario occurs, in which that collared sheep reaches the flock that has been driven away. If this should occur, the handler must retrieve the entire group that the collared sheep joined and begin the task anew. This can quickly eat up many of the points allotted for the international shed! However, the handler should stay focused on the task, not grow discouraged, and remember that being able to accomplish the task and then to proceed to the pen is also important to a competitive overall score.

Here, the range and sophistication of your training program becomes evident. Imagine that, of the twenty sheep, eight are grazing peacefully some distance away, and you split off two more; but a collared sheep darts in and leaves with them. As this smaller group moves toward the larger flock, you must be able to "unlock" your dog from the group he is holding, and turn him back toward the group of three sheep that are leaving. But, in addition, the dog must understand, or be able to be told, that he is not to bring back all eleven sheep, but only the closer group of three. Many dogs kick out and want to bring all of the sheep back; a command that will bring the dog in can save the handler from having to begin the entire task anew.

Another situation that can arise is a collared sheep who is extremely anxious to leave. This sheep can create real problems, always moving toward the front of the flock, always trying to attach itself to another sheep. Managing this

♠ FROM THE HANDLER'S POST ♠

situation is a real test of the handler's stockmanship. While as a general rule the handler would like all of the sheep to be facing constantly in the direction of the imaginary chute, in this case that single sheep needs to be turned back, to be discouraged from continuing to attempt to escape. Either the dog or the handler—or the two together—can accomplish this task. Subtle movements, eye contact, etc., are the only possible tools. It should be remembered that if much aggression is used on that one sheep, it can alarm the others, creating further problems; and if the dog and handler concentrate too much on turning back that one sheep, others may escape in the meantime. The real key to the international shed is having the sheep not quite realize that they are being separated at all; but one rebellious collared sheep can create the need for stronger interference.

One undesirable situation that can arise is to end up with six sheep in the ring—five collared and one uncollared. As mentioned earlier, the ideal shed involves two or three sheep in the final sort; this creates an easier situation. But it is not always possible, and you may have to take your sorts where you can get them. Once you are faced with having to separate one single sheep from the other five, you must at all costs avoid alarming that single sheep. You must allow it to feel invisible, while you concentrate your attention on the ones that you would like *not* to leave the ring. As soon as the uncollared sheep shows the slightest interest in leaving to join its fellows outside the ring, a subtle movement by either the handler or the dog should encourage the single in that direction, while calmly and deliberately stopping the others from following suit. A very small hole, if managed correctly, can quickly become a big enough hole for the handler to ease in and drive that single away. Handlers should not become over-anxious and move too quickly at this point, or that single sheep might decide that it is afraid to make the solo journey toward the more distant flock. Rather, as we have discussed, the sheep should feel as if it is making its own decision, and can make good its escape, without the dog and handler watching, pushing, or threatening it in any way.

As the number of sheep remaining in the ring decreases, it is increasingly important for dog, handler, and sheep to maintain their composure. The shed becomes a game of balance; the handler steps back when necessary to release pressure, the dog is asked to move back to release pressure or asked to come in one or two steps, and the entire flock is thus persuaded to stay or to go without alarm.

♠ FROM THE HANDLER'S POST ♠

Additionally, the calming tactics of the "horse whisperer" should be used. The handler can use a lot of subtle aids such as eye contact, facing or turning away from a particular sheep, and other modes of communication that are almost invisible to onlookers. Dogs that have practiced this task develop similar ways of applying or releasing subtle pressure, in response to what the handler is doing. It is helpful if the dog can be moved slowly, quietly, and deliberately; all the while, the intention is that the sheep not be aware that they are being controlled and maneuvered. It might be said that while other aspects of the trial competition are a "science," the international shed is more of an "art." More animals are involved than in a traditional shed; more things can go wrong; more factors must be taken into account; and both handler and dog simply must develop a feel for what needs to be done at each particular moment of each international shed.

All of these talents, which are very difficult to put into words, are developed in only one way: practice. As we mentioned earlier, the international shed is one of the most sophisticated tests of teamwork, of a working relationship, that has been developed through hours and miles of practice reading stock and reading each other. All the practice in the world will not have taught the dog and handler how this particular group of sheep will behave; but practice does hone the perceptive abilities and the subtle communication methods necessary to accomplish the international shed. The dog that understands the task, that holds his distance off the sheep, and that stays where he is told to stay, is the one that can get this job done.

The international shed is a part only of the most advanced level of stockdog trialing. However, practicing the international shed can not only have real farm work applications and improve your dog's level of education and talent, but can also be a great deal of fun. Of course, collars are not necessary for practicing the international shed at home. What is necessary is for the handler to set up a plan and then to execute that plan, without changing his intentions mid-stream. For example, the handler might decide to separate all black-faced sheep from the others; or sort out the spotted sheep; or mix together a group of hair sheep and wool sheep and then sort them back out. But it is important for the handler to decide ahead of time how many sheep and which sheep will be the "marked" ones, and then not to allow himself to sidestep the task or take shortcuts.

The international shed as a whole can and should be practiced in this way, with dogs that have reached the appropriate level of training.

♠ FROM THE HANDLER'S POST ♠

However, individual elements of the international shed can and should be taught much earlier in the training program, so that once you and your dog are ready to perform the international shed, the dog already has accumulated certain abilities and lessons that can now be put to use in a different way.

Since the earliest stages, the handler who is attentive to building a good, solid training program has already been getting the young dog accustomed to coming through a large group of sheep. So, by the time you are ready to practice for the international shed, the dog should already be used to taking the sheep on the head, working into their faces, and working quietly and deliberately.

Another essential element to a good training foundation is automatic obedience and unquestioning trust on the part of the dog. A dog that is flexible and fluid will be able to master this task, but hesitation on the part of the dog will allow the wrong sheep to get past, or will stop a sheep just when you are ready to release it. Your training program should not repeat the same exercises, thus allowing the dog to create habits and to react automatically. Rather, a training program that encompasses variety and some surprises will teach the dog to watch constantly for cues from the handler, and to execute commands quickly.

Finally, a general requirement for being able to execute the international shed at the end of a strenuous course is the dog's physical fitness. Particularly with the added stress of an international-style course, a dog needs to be in peak physical condition in order to perform this task. Dogs that are trained for only ten or fifteen minutes at a time will often lose their stamina just when they need to be able to catch a sheep or respond quickly. In order to be fair to the dog, handlers should prepare for this kind of course over a period of weeks and make sure that they are not asking more than the dog will be able to give.

As stated above, training for the international shed happens a piece at a time; it may be several months before all of the pieces can be put together. One important piece of the training for the international shed is teaching the dog *not* to come all the way through the space that is created. Dogs who have been trained only for the traditional shed all too often learn to anticipate it and to move very quickly once they see a hole open up. This can be counterproductive once you get to the international shed. Therefore, one exercise to practice is creating a hole and then not having the dog come in at all, or having him come in only slightly. Or you can create a hole, then allow that hole to close and create a different hole.

♠ FROM THE HANDLER'S POST ♠

All of these variations teach the dog to be patient, to be attentive to signals from the handler, and to function as part of a team rather than working always out of habit.

Another piece of this puzzle is teaching the dog to stay where you have left him, holding the sheep that have been cut off. Too often, handlers who are training for a trial accomplish the shed and then immediately call the dog off, or ask him to round up all of the sheep again. The international shed is a longer and more involved task that requires the dog to work in multiple steps and phases. This is an ability that must be taught, consciously and conscientiously. As part of the training, the handler should set up a shed, and then actively drive one group away while asking the dog to hold the remaining sheep for a longer period of time than usual. This can be done quickly, can break up habits and routines in the training program, teaches the dog a valuable skill, and does not require a "rehearsal" of the entire international shed. Piece by piece, your dog will be accumulating the elements needed to put together the final task, and you will be increasingly able to trust the dog and turn your back on him with confidence.

Finally, the dog needs to be able to do a "partial re-gathering" of the sheep—in other words, to bring back the sheep that have just escaped without flanking out to regroup the entire flock. The dog needs to have a "come in" whistle or command that will bring him through a space and turn him on a few sheep, even if they are some distance away from the handler. This can be taught if you have enough sheep to divide them into three groups. First, split the sheep, and drive the first group off, or allow them to leave on their own. Then split the remaining sheep into two groups, having your dog hold the rear group as the middle group moves off toward the first group, those that are furthest away. Before the middle group moves too far away, ask the dog to turn from the sheep he is holding, and then have him bring back the middle group but not the far group. Once taught, this "come in" command may have several other applications besides the international shed, but it is an essential weapon in your arsenal for the occasions when the wrong sheep escape from the ring. Soon the dog will learn to stay alert, ready—in case he is asked—to catch just the sheep that bolt past him, and he will begin to understand the difference between the traditional shed and a true "sorting" of the sheep.

Once the trainer is fairly comfortable that his dog has mastered these essential "partial skills," he is ready to put it all together and to practice the complex task of sorting sheep. At this point, the training is as much for the handler as for

♠ FROM THE HANDLER'S POST ♠

the dog, and even experienced handlers need to hone their skills before heading to this level of competition. Handlers should be diligent in not settling for "easy shots" or "lucky breaks" during practice. Instead, they should repeat the set-up again and again until they can make things happen, until they are acting rather than merely reacting. Only through repeated practice can you and your dog be ready to respond quickly when the unexpected happens.

Moderation is always critical. Too much practice of the international shed can be detrimental to your dog's quick response during the traditional shed; too much automatic repetition of the traditional shed can make your dog less flexible or less trusting when you ask for something more complicated. Flexible and pliable dogs are the direct result of training programs that incorporate a variety of skills and tasks. The international shed is not one job, but rather it represents the accumulation of many different abilities, and their smooth integration by a focused and perceptive handler. This is the reason that the international shed is incorporated only at the highest level of stockdog trialing, and why in many ways it represents the greatest achievement in terms of stockmanship and teamwork.

As in so many aspects of life, preparation and flexibility are the keys to success on the trial field; anticipate that you will need all of the tools available to you once you step onto that field. Practice for as many variables as possible, including the possibility that you may find yourself competing in a double lift championship someday. Ready your dog(s) for these possibilities. Travel as much as you can to experience terrain and sheep different from your own. Question those whose dogs or runs you respect and/or admire. Over my many years of training and trialing these amazing dogs, each new field or flock of sheep, each time to the post or to work on the farm, expanded my vocabulary and taught me something new. And each time I worked with these dogs in this way, my sense of wonder at the beauty of this sport and the abilities of the border collie was renewed.

www.ingramcontent.com/pod-product-compliance
Lightning Source LLC
Chambersburg PA
CBHW070609300426
44113CB00010B/1475